KEEPERS
OF THE TOTEM

✜

This volume is one of a series that chronicles the history and culture of the Native Americans. Other books in the series include:

The Cover: Nathan Jackson, a contemporary Tlingit artist, wears a traditional button blanket and a Raven crest dance headdress that he designed and carved. Behind him stretch the Tongass Narrows and surrounding hills near Ketchikan, Alaska, part of the Tlingits' ancient homeland.

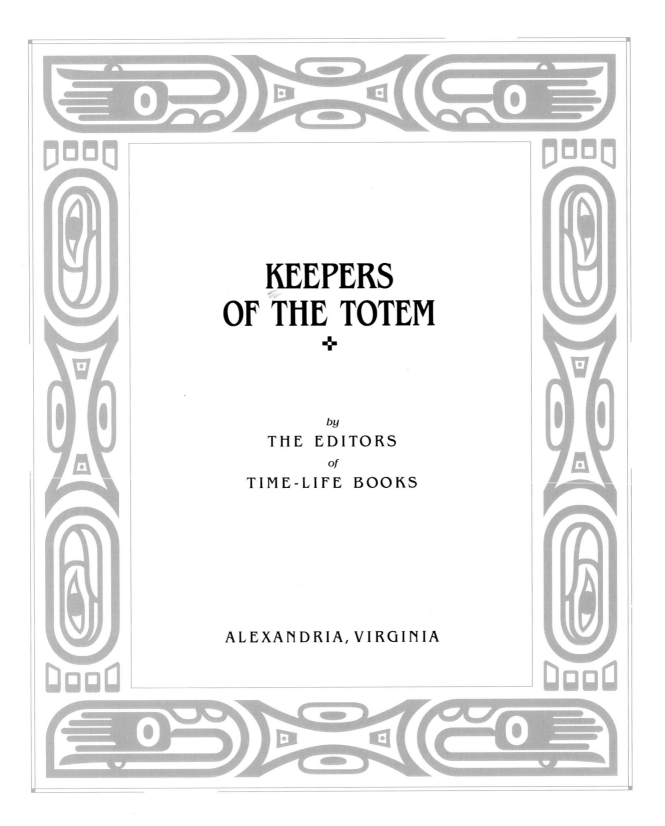

KEEPERS
OF THE TOTEM

✥

by
THE EDITORS
of
TIME-LIFE BOOKS

ALEXANDRIA, VIRGINIA

979.5
KEE

© 1993 Time Life Inc. All rights reserved.
No part of this book may be reproduced in any form
or by any electronic or mechanical means, including
information storage and retrieval devices or systems,
without prior written permission from the publisher,
except that brief passages may be quoted for reviews.
First printing. Printed in U.S.A.
Published simultaneously in Canada.
School and library distribution by Silver Burdett
Company, Morristown, New Jersey 07960.

Time-Life is a trademark of Time Warner Inc. U.S.A.

Library of Congress Cataloging in Publication Data
Keepers of the totem/by the editors of Time-
Life Books.
    p. cm. — (The American Indians)
    Includes bibliographical references and index.
    ISBN 0-8094-9558-9
    ISBN 0-8094-9559-7 (lib. bdg.)
    1. Indians of North America—Northwest Coast of
North America—Social life and customs.
    2. Indians of North America—Northwest Coast of
North America—History.
    I. Time-Life Books. II. Series.
E78.N78K44 · 1993   93-24361
979.5′00497—dc20   CIP

THE AMERICAN INDIANS

General Consultants
Frederick E. Hoxie is director of the D'Arcy McNickle
Center for the History of the American Indian at the
Newberry Library in Chicago. Dr. Hoxie is the author
of *A Final Promise: The Campaign to Assimilate the
Indians 1880-1920* and other works. He has served
as a history consultant to the Cheyenne River and
Standing Rock Sioux tribes, Little Big Horn College
archives, and the Senate Select Committee on Indian
Affairs. He is a trustee of the National Museum of the
American Indian in Washington, D.C.

Jay Miller is an anthropologist and linguist who has
taught in the Native Language Teacher Program for
Tsimshian and Haida in Prince Rupert, British Columbia. He has been a research associate and director of
the American Indian Studies Program at the University of Washington and editor and assistant director at
the D'Arcy McNickle Center for the History of the
American Indian at the Newberry Library. As part of
his lifelong involvement with Native Americans, Dr.
Miller has been tutored by the elders of many North
American tribes, including the Delaware, Salish,
Creek, and Tsimshian, and has participated in their
rituals. He has also written numerous articles about
Native Americans for professional journals and is the
author of several books, among them *Shamanic Od-
yssey: Lushootseed Salish Journey to the Land of the
Dead, The Tsimshian and Their Neighbors of the
North Pacific Coast,* and *Earthmaker: Tribal Stories
from Native North America.*

Special Consultants
Steve Brown is Assistant Curator of Native American
Art at the Seattle Art Museum. An artist and writer
involved in Northwest Coast studies for more than 25
years, Mr. Brown was one of the principal artists who
replicated the Chief Shake's House posts, originally
carved by Kajisdoo'akch. His writings include "From
Taguan to Klukwan," which traces the work of an
early Tlingit master artist and which appeared in *Faces, Voices and Dreams,* the centennial catalog of the
Sheldon Jackson Museum in Sitka, Alaska.

Jim Hart is an artist and descendant of the Eden-
shaws, an aristocratic Haida family, many of whose
members were known for their artistic accomplish-
ments. After learning to make woodcarving tools
from the noted carver Robert Davidson, Mr. Hart
worked for Bill Reid, the grand master of large contemporary Haida sculpture. Subsequently, Mr. Hart
has created a large number of sculptures and other
works for corporations, individuals, and public institutions, among them a Dogfish Dance screen for the
Provincial Museum in Victoria, British Columbia, and
numerous totem poles, including a 30-foot totem
pole for Old Kings Southern Castle in Halsingborg,
Sweden. Mr. Hart has also designed and supervised
the construction of many old Haida houses using
time-honored techniques.

C. 1

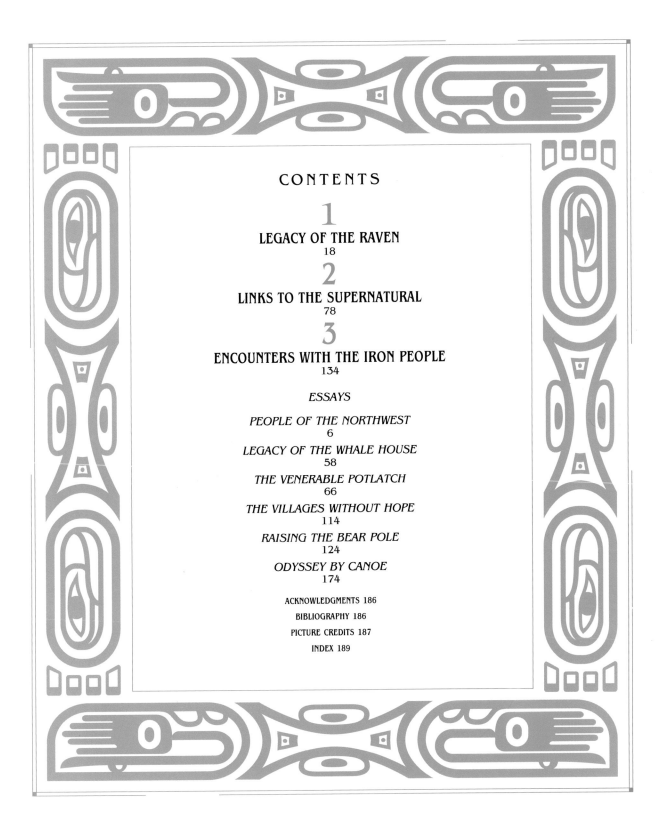

CONTENTS

1

LEGACY OF THE RAVEN

2

LINKS TO THE SUPERNATURAL

3

ENCOUNTERS WITH THE IRON PEOPLE

PEOPLE OF THE NORTHWEST

"Every part of this soil is sacred in the estimation of my people," said Chief Seattle of the Suquamish and Duwamish tribes in 1853, when asked to sell his land to the United States government.

Indeed, this land had always proved a divine benefactor. For thousands of years, Seattle's people and neighboring Kwakiutl, Nootka, Haida, Tsimshian, Tlingit, and other groups had thrived along the rich and varied coastline that stretched from southeastern Alaska to northern Washington State. During the warm months, the region's teeming waterways and abundant forests provided enough food and material goods to sustain the people year-round. Thus freed from want, they could devote the winter months to elaborate ceremonies that celebrated the spirits of both the bountiful earth and ancestors long past but still powerful. Despite the changes and hardships wrought by the arrival of whites, these traditions endured, and the ancient seasonal cycle of life continues.

Photographed in 1881, totem poles carved with clan crests tower above cedar-plank houses at Massett, a Haida village on the Queen Charlotte Islands in British Columbia.

Tlingit guests in Sitka, Alaska, wear traditional dance costumes in preparation for a potlatch, a celebration featuring lavish feasts and gift giving. These events, held to mark a naming, a marriage, or a death, usually began with several days of singing and dancing competitions between clans.

Poised to thrust, a Kwakiutl man spearfishes for salmon from a hand-carved cedar canoe at Quatsino on northern Vancouver Island, British Columbia. Fish—fresh, dried, smoked, or otherwise preserved—were dietary staples as well as important trade items for the peoples of the Northwest Coast.

Wearing masks representing animal spirits, Kwakiutl dancers perform at a winter ceremony in a photograph taken by Edward Curtis in 1910. The Kwakiutl believe that spirits take over the bodies of the dancers during the rite and imbue those mortals with awesome powers.

In a photograph taken late in the 19th century, Indian women and children of the Northwest Coast wait at a train station in Vancouver, British Columbia. Indian women skilled in processing and preserving fish went to work in canneries after whites established commercial fishing ventures.

Photographed in 1884, the Kwakiutl village of Newitti shows evidence of the native peoples' adaptations to the arrival of white settlers. A sign above the door of one cedar-plank house reads: CHEAP...The Home of the Head Chief of All Tribes in This Country. White Man Can [Get] Information. The other sign says: He Is True and Honest. He Don't Give No Trouble to No White Man.

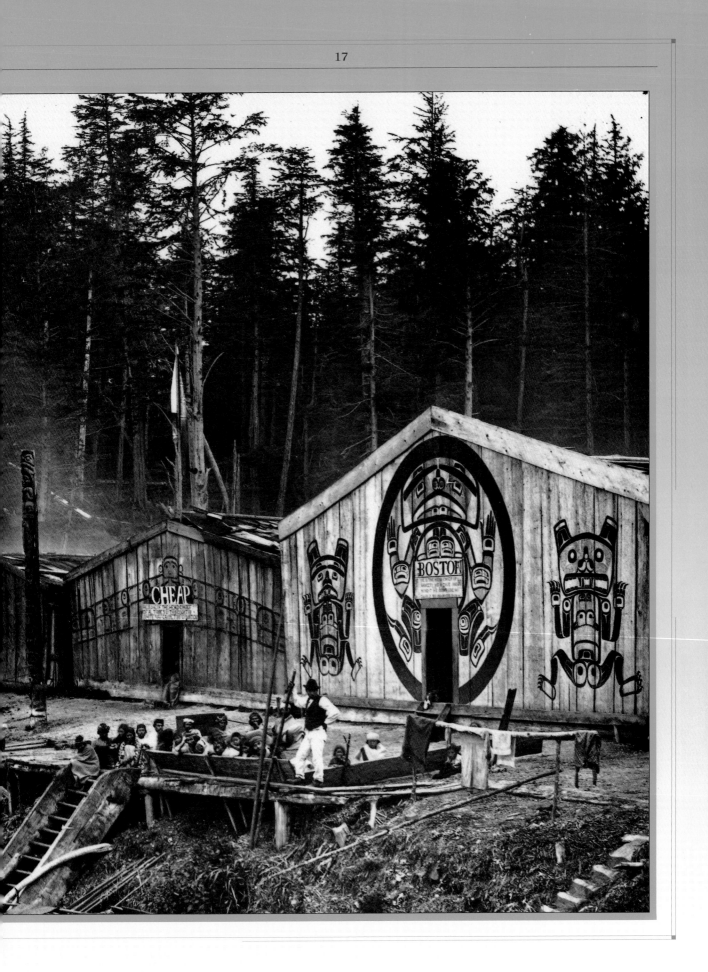

1

LEGACY OF THE RAVEN

Raven watched over the harbor. Painted boldly across the front of a 60-foot-wide cedar-plank house, the fabled bird, bringer of light to the world, gazed out across the water of a sheltered inlet on the coast of the Pacific Northwest. In Raven's great beak nestled the moon—a sign to all who paddled into the bay that this mighty house belonged to the wealthy Tsimshian chief, Raven in the Moonlight. It was the only house in the village so magnificently emblazoned; and it easily dwarfed all other structures along the shore, a clear indication of Raven in the Moonlight's exalted status.

On this winter's evening, dozens of large cedar canoes were drawn up on the beach under Raven's eye. The vessels had arrived from villages up and down the shore bearing men and women of high rank along with their relatives and slaves. All were gathered at Raven in the Moonlight's house for a potlatch, a traditional feast and gift-giving ceremony.

Inside the great house, the guests looked on as masked figures danced around a fire to the pounding of box drums and the chanting of singers. Raven in the Moonlight and the invited chiefs sat in the place of honor—a platform at the rear of the house, erected in front of a decorated wooden screen. Carved and painted on the screen was a scene from the sacred history of the house, one in which Raven assumed the guise of a mischievous infant in the house of a spirit chief and stole from him the light that became the sun, the moon, and the stars. A small round opening in the center of the screen led into a cubicle where the treasures of the house were normally kept. On this night, however, the cubicle lay empty. All its treasures—masks, ceremonial bowls, ornamental blankets, wooden helmets, engraved sheets of copper, and other prized items handed down by the host's ancestors—had been placed on the platform in front of the screen for the guests to admire.

Abruptly, the music and dancing stopped, and a close kinsman of Raven in the Moonlight, chosen by him to serve as speaker, rose to address the guests. He boasted of his ancestors and, as was the custom, belittled those of his guests. He then presented the invited chiefs with a

A totem pole portraying heroes of the Raven Clan (left) stands before the vivid facade of a Tlingit house in Alaska (above). Among Northwest Coast Indians, animal designs were used by wealthy families as crests that, displayed in front of a house, proclaimed the pedigree of the owner.

regional delicacy, heaping ladles of oil from the eulachon, or candlefish, mixed with snow carried down from nearby mountaintops. As the chiefs consumed the rich mixture, several of Raven in the Moonlight's warriors rushed into the house, making menacing gestures. The chiefs did not flinch. They knew that both the overgenerous offering of oil and the threats of the warriors were in keeping with the spirit of the occasion, which combined keen competitiveness with unbridled hospitality.

Soon the warriors ceased their hostile movements and scattered eagle down over the heads of the guests as a sign of peace. Now was the time for the gift giving to commence. While his people sang songs that praised the greatness of his house, Raven in the Moonlight directed the distribution of the presents—blankets, bundles of food, and for the highest-ranking guests, such finely wrought articles as cedar boxes and canoes. From time to time, speakers rose to joke about the shortcomings of some of the visitors. More and more goods were brought out and placed before the guests. The pile of gifts grew ever higher, until the roof boards had to be removed. No one could say that these keepers of the Raven crest were not great and generous.

As the gift giving neared its conclusion, Raven in the Moonlight's uncle stood up to address the gathering. "Raven in the Moonlight has asked me to speak to you about his ancestors and the sacred history of his house," he explained. "We all know that Raven was a powerful spirit who came from the sky as a shining youth. Here on earth he learned to eat food and became ravenously hungry. He would do anything to get food, and sometimes he did things that have helped us to this day. He gave us fish and game. He taught us to respect other creatures. He taught us to honor Heaven Above. But more than these, he brought us out of darkness. He got light for us." The uncle then related the story of how Raven took light from the house of a spirit chief in a box and broke the container open, freeing everyone from perpetual gloom.

"All people admire the work of Raven," the speaker went on, "but the people of the Raven Clan are particularly close to him. In this house, where you are being fed and entertained, they honor the Moon as a special gift of Raven. This is because, ages ago, a woman of this house was lost in the forest. She was high-class and knew how to take care of herself. She prayed constantly and made offerings, although she had almost nothing. Just when she thought she would die, she received a great gift, one that she brought into this house. It was late when she came upon a stream in the woods. A full moon shone on the water and allowed her to

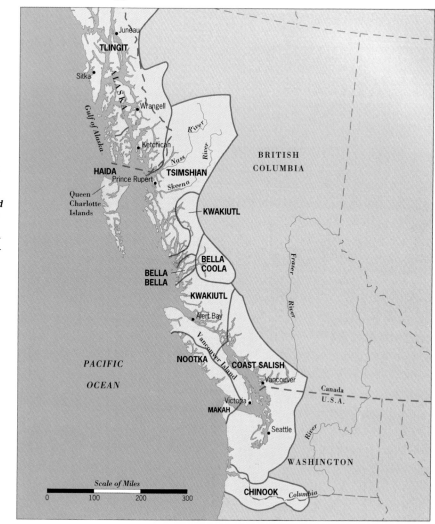

Stretching from Yakutat Bay in Alaska to the Columbia River in Oregon, a narrow strip of coastline and a string of rugged offshore island chains have for centuries been home to the various peoples known collectively as Northwest Coast Indians. Separated from one another by dense forest and myriad waterways, each group developed its own distinct culture. What these native peoples shared, however, was a knack for thriving in a bountiful environment as well as a prodigious gift for art and ceremony.

see many salmon swimming there. These salmon saved her from starving. The next day, she followed the stream to the shore and discovered where she was. In a short time, she was home. She told the story to her people, and they went back to the stream, where they caught many fish. Today the house of Raven in the Moonlight still owns this stream, and you have eaten many of the salmon that are still found there. That is a sacred history of the house of Raven in the Moonlight."

The host chief and his kin then exhibited the treasures of the house and told the story of each in turn. More gift giving, singing, and storytelling ensued. When the last present had been handed out, the visiting chiefs rose one by one to offer elaborate speeches of thanks to Raven in the Moonlight and to confirm the prestige of his house. Then they returned to their canoes with their followers and headed home, laden with gifts. By lavishing wealth on others, the household of Raven in the Moonlight had done much to distinguish itself. For the chief and his people knew that all bounty in the world came as a gift from Raven and other ancestral powers, and only through lavish feats of generosity could they prove that they were worthy descendants of those magnanimous spirits.

The glow of a sunset warms an evergreen-cloaked archipelago near Sitka, Alaska. The moist climate of the Pacific Northwest nourished dense forests that supplied the region's Indians with wood for houses and bark for garments. For food, they turned to the ocean and inland rivers and streams for fish, and to the forests for game.

The custom of bringing honor to one's house or lineage through gift giving was just one of a number of traditions that linked the Tsimshian—who made their homes along the northern shores of present-day British Columbia—to other Native American peoples of the Northwest Coast. These groups, with their great houses and noble crests, or totems, were products of a unique environment, a lush corridor of ocean waters and forested shores extending for a distance of approximately 1,500 miles from the broad mouth of the Columbia River in the south to the glacial inlets of the Alaska Panhandle in the north.

Along much of that stretch, volcanic upheaval had forged a mountainous barrier between the coast and the interior, so that the tribes that were living on either side of the peaks communicated only with difficulty and evolved distinct customs. More than just a cultural divide, the mountains favored the coastal corridor by wringing out moisture sweeping in from the ocean on prevailing westerly winds. In many harbors, 100 inches of rain would fall annually—and some spots received two or three times that amount. The damp climate dismayed later intruders from sunny climes but agreed with natives of the coast, who knew that water brought them wealth and vitality. The myriad rivers and bays teemed with fish and marine mammals that nourished the people, while the mists shrouding the forests promoted the growth of great trees that offered villagers abundant shelter, fuel, fiber, and transport.

Mindful of this legacy, some peoples of the Northwest Coast traced their very origins to the margins of the sea. According to a legend handed down by the Haida, who settled west of the Tsimshian on the Queen Charlotte Islands (Haida Gwaii), the first of their ancestors were coaxed into the world on a desolate beach by Raven himself, who was prowling the shore on his own when he came upon a partially open clamshell. Raven was all alone in the world at the time, and eager for company. Bending down to examine the clamshell, he noticed a small face peering timidly out at him. "Come out! Come out!" Raven called. Several more small faces soon peeked out from the edge of the shell. Slowly, shyly, the tiny people pushed open the clamshell and climbed out onto the sandy shore. These were the original Haida—the People, as they called themselves—and they emerged from the same watery element that later sustained their descendants.

As this legend suggests, the Haida have occupied their homeland since time immemorial. Archaeological evidence indicates that the Queen Charlotte Islands were settled at least 10,000 years ago. Occupa-

KWAKIUTL CHIEF

COAST SALISH WOMAN

tion of the region as a whole began when the intermittent glaciers that once isolated the Northwest Coast from the heart of the continent had retreated sufficiently to allow migratory bands to populate the area. Some coast dwellers in the southern part of the region evidently reached the shores of present-day Oregon and Washington State from the interior through passes carved by rivers swollen with glacial melt. Mightiest of those waterways was the Columbia River, and the avenue it formed would continue to lure migrants to the verdant coast from the semiarid hinterland for ages to come. To the north, other bands would make their way through the imposing coastal range to the Pacific by following the course of the surging Fraser and Skeena rivers.

Not all of the groups who settled the Northwest Coast moved overland, however. Thanks to the presence of barrier islands that extended with few breaks all the way from southeastern Alaska to Washington State's Olympic Peninsula, the coastal waters were generally protected enough to be traversed by canoe. This long skein of sheltered waterways served not only as an early migration route but also as an enduring trade route, linking the coastal cultures to the Far North and thence to Siberia. All Native Americans could claim distant ties to Asia, but the Asiatic influence was particularly strong among peoples of the Pacific Northwest. European navigators who began visiting the region in the late 1700s were struck by similarities in appearance and customs between the Indians there and the inhabitants of coastal Siberia and Japan.

The variety of ornaments and clothing depicted in these portraits, taken about 1900, indicates the cultural richness and diversity of Pacific Northwest peoples. More than 25 different languages were spoken in the region, which was home to dozens of tribes.

NOOTKA CHIEF   TLINGIT SHAMAN

Of the various peoples who shared in the rich ceremonial traditions of the totems, those closest to Asia geographically if not culturally were the Tlingit of southeastern Alaska. Theirs was a harsh setting. Winter winds drove sleet and snow against the planks of the big houses, and the sheer incline of the coastal range made treks inland to trade or hunt arduous in any season. Floating ice and strong tides challenged paddlers stalking seals or sea otters, and hunters on land faced an incalculable foe: the grizzly bear. When a Tlingit ran afoul of a grizzly and was mauled to death, his kinsmen regarded it as an affront from a powerful, competing clan and settled the score by claiming the life of a bear in return—making sure as they did so to pay ritual homage to their prey, whom they respected as much as they feared. Conditioned to such rigors, the Tlingit were formidable warriors, rendered all the more intimidating by the wooden helmets and masks they wore in battle, carved with fierce images of their supernatural protectors.

South of the Tlingit along the mainland resided the Tsimshian, whose settlements extended well inland from the coast along the estuaries of the Skeena and Nass rivers. Long before white merchants arrived to promote the fur trade, Tsimshians were venturing up those waterways to offer landlocked tribes bounty from the sea in return for pelts and other goods. The Tsimshian had an uneasy relationship with their distant offshore neighbors, the Haida, with whom they traded and sometimes tangled. By necessity, the Haida were adventurous mariners, whose trips

NOOTKA WOMAN   TLINGIT SHAMAN

across the broad Hecate Strait took them out of sight of land and exposed them to rough waters. Soon after their first contacts with Europeans, they added canvas sails to their long canoes to speed the journey. A white visitor to the Tsimshian later marveled at the approach of a fleet of about 40 Haida canoes, with white sails spread on either side, flying shoreward "like immense birds or butterflies."

Farther south, on the northeastern coast of Vancouver Island and the adjoining mainland, lay the realm of the Kwakiutl (Kwakwaka'wakw). Flanking a strait that narrowed in places to a distance of less than a mile, the Kwakiutl dominated the crucial inland passage between populous Puget Sound and the northern harbors of the Tsimshian, Haida, and Tlingit. The Kwakiutl often exploited that position by attacking those voyagers that they deemed hostile and exacting tribute from others. In time, their knack for acquiring wealth and devoting it to competitive displays of rank made them outstanding exponents of the potlatch.

West of the Kwakiutl, on the windward side of Vancouver Island, lived the Nootka (Nuuchanulth), who faced open sea just beyond their home harbors. The challenge of navigating ocean swells made the Nootka master canoe builders, whose vessels were sought in trade by distant groups. Southernmost of the Nootkans were the peoples who settled on the Olympic Peninsula, notably the Makah, who supplemented their fishing and foraging with whale hunting.

The sheltered waters extending southward from Kwakiutl territory to

COAST SALISH BOY　　　　　　　　　　　　**HAIDA WOMAN**

the lower end of Puget Sound were the domain of the Coast Salish. Like the other major groups, the Coast Salish were linked by language and custom but divided into many small tribes. In their case, the tribes were quite distinct, with dialects that differed markedly from one inlet to the next. Compared with the peoples to their north, the Coast Salish were less elaborate in their ceremonies and less rigid in their social structure.

Occupying the southern segment of the Northwest Coast cultural zone were the Chinook, masters of the Columbia River valley. Their social network ranged even farther inland than the Tsimshian, and their trading ties were more extensive. The Chinook served as middlemen not only between the shore and the interior but also between the northern and central Pacific Coast. It was through their hands, for example, that prized dentalium shells gathered along the beaches of Vancouver Island reached tribes in California, where the shells served as currency.

For all their variety, the peoples who settled the Northwest Coast drew on common resources and exploited their assets in similar ways, evolving prosperous households whose members lived together in imposing lodges and devoted considerable time and energy to dramatic rituals. Even though contact with whites exposed these proud peoples to profound changes, they managed to preserve many of their traditions, and their cultures remain very much alive today in scores of small villages up and down the coast. Now as in the past, the keepers of the totems draw sustenance and inspiration for their ceremonies of praise and gift giving from Nature's own displays of generosity—miracles of renewal that fill the waters and forests with offerings for the people and reaffirm their age-old belief that bountiful spirits were the founders of their families.

The traditional way of life along the Northwest Coast was marked by seasonal movement, as people ventured from one site to another in pursuit of food. All of the tribes had winter villages, but from spring through fall, households periodically packed up their essential belongings and made lengthy forays. Among the Tsimshian, the first of these annual moves came as early as February or March, when people left villages near the coast and headed for fishing camps located up the Nass River, where the eulachon began to swarm even before the river was clear of ice. Part of the catch was consumed on the spot by hungry Tsimshians, who had been living on dried fish for much of the winter and were eager for fresh food. But most of the eulachon they harvested was rendered for oil—a process that involved leaving the fish to ripen in covered pits for several days, then boiling the decaying flesh in water and allowing the mixture to settle so that the oil collected at the surface. Sometimes Indians used their own canoes as cauldrons, filling the vessels with water and tossing in red-hot stones along with the fish to bring the ripe brew to a boil.

The pungent, nutrient-rich liquid that emerged from this process served the Indians of the Northwest as their essential seasoning. Stored in sealed wooden boxes or in the hollow stems of kelp, the oil was commonly used with dried fish, roots, or berries to round out an otherwise lean diet. Since heavy eulachon runs were few and far between, many coastal groups traded with the Tsimshian for the oil. Surpluses were exchanged with inland tribes at the far end of trade routes that were aptly referred to as "grease trails."

The eulachon is so important to the Tsimshian that they call it the "savior" fish—indeed, when they were exposed to Christianity, the word they used to refer to Christ was their word for eulachon. But many other creatures from the sea helped sustain the coastal peoples as a whole. Mollusks, dug from mud flats at low tide, were culled so assiduously by Indians of the region down through the centuries that imposing mounds of discarded shells marked the sites of ancient settlements. No less prolific were the herring that swarmed up many inlets in such numbers each spring that they could literally be raked from the water's surface with long

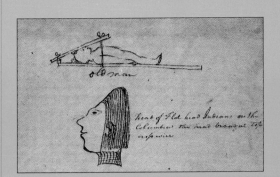

A Haida cradleboard (below) features a cedar-bark pad that, when lashed snugly against the brow, molded a baby's head. A detail from a sketch by William Clark (left) shows another type of carrier in which the head was pressed between boards.

Their elongated heads marking them as members of the elite, a number of Kwakiutl women watch admiringly as a mother tends to her infant daughter in a cradleboard. A pad has been strapped across the baby's head in order to flatten and lengthen it.

MARKING THE ELITE

Describing women he encountered among the Chinook Indians, the 19th-century explorer William Clark commented, "The most remarkable trait in their physiognomy is the peculiar flatness and width of the forehead." Peculiar as it was to outsiders, a woman's flat, backward-sloping forehead was for centuries a sign of noble rank in many Northwest Coast tribes. The distortion was created by strapping an infant into a cradleboard rigged to apply gentle but constant pressure to its malleable skull to create the desired peaked shape. Apparently the procedure was painless and caused no mental impairment.

poles equipped with bone teeth. A single sweep of the rake caught as many as a dozen herring, which served both as food for people and as bait for larger prey like the halibut. That bottom dweller was snared with a special V-shaped wooden hook, barbed at one end with bone and carved at the other end with an image that lured the quarry with spirit power. Among the Kwakiutl, a fisherman would refer to this hook as his "younger brother" and cover it with fresh bait as an offering to the halibut, whom he addressed as "old woman." As he played out his line, he would pray to her to accept the gift: "Go on, old woman! Crawl up to it. Now it is well prepared. This is your sweet food."

No creature inhabiting the waters meant more to Indians of the area, however, than the salmon, which at one time or another during the warmer months staged spectacular spawning runs up virtually every inlet of the Northwest Coast. Altogether, there were five species in the region—chinook, sockeye, humpback, coho, and dog salmon—and the Indians knew them intimately. According to a legend of the Tlingit that was shared by native peoples throughout the region, the five species constituted distinct clans and lived in their own villages beyond the horizon. Each spring, the five clans would gather for a great meeting before setting out in their invisible canoes for their summer spawning grounds. The clans embarked on the journey together, but invariably the lowly dog salmon, acting out of spite and jealousy, broke up the canoes of the coho salmon, which is why the cohos would always arrive later in the year.

To catch the powerful halibut, the Makah of northwest Washington State used a hook (below) made from a straight piece of fir or hemlock that was softened by steam, bent into a curve, and then tipped with a three-inch-long bone barb secured with spruce root and pine pitch. To ensure a good catch, Makah fishermen prayed to their hooks.

Whenever they occurred, salmon runs prompted entire households to leave their villages and move to prescribed fishing grounds, which their chiefs claimed by inheritance. Like the spawning runs that inspired them, these purposeful migrations of men, women, and children deeply impressed the region's early white explorers, who witnessed canoe after canoe, laden with household goods, heading upstream to the fishing camps: "Indians in swarms proceeding to the fishery above," reported one observer along the Fraser River in the early 1800s. No less impressive were

About 1900 a Makah woman cleans halibut at Neah Bay in Washington State. During the summer, the men of the tribe brought in thousands of pounds of the fish daily. Although the Makah dried most of their catch and stored it for their own use, selling some of the fish to white traders and settlers proved to be a lucrative source of cash beginning in the mid-1800s.

the sundry techniques used by the Indians to harvest the salmon. In the words of one white surveyor who traveled widely in northern British Columbia and Alaska during the 19th century, "There is little in the art of fishing we can teach these Indians."

The peoples who lived along the coast caught the first salmon of the season with hook and line, as the fish congregated in bays or inlets before starting off on their strenuous runs upstream. Nootka fishermen employed an ingenious means of trolling for the salmon that gathered in Friendly Cove: They fastened lines to their paddles, which enabled them to propel their canoes and lure their quarry, all in one motion. Traditionally, the hooks used by Indians of the region for trolling were fashioned from wood, bone, or stone, while the lines were made from bull kelp, whale sinew, intertwined strands of cedar bark, or even human hair. Coast Salish fishermen, for example, favored slender lines of woven human hair that were all but invisible to fish—which was one reason Coast Salish women were expected to let their locks grow as long as possible.

When the salmon began their spawning run, the Indians set aside hooks and lines and resorted to artfully crafted devices that could snare many fish at a time—including nets of cedar bark or nettle fiber that were cast by hand or strung out between canoes; long basket traps that tapered toward the closed end, stranding the fish; and elaborate weirs, or fences, designed to guide the salmon toward basket traps or other enclosures where they could be readily taken with nets or spears. Although a small weir crossing a narrow stream or estuary might be owned and operated by a single household, a larger weir spanning a major river required the cooperative effort of an entire village, with each household claiming its share of the harvest.

Like other subsistence activities, salmon fishing was surrounded with rituals designed to appease the spirit of the prey and ensure that the salmon clans would return to their spawning grounds year after year. Special honor was granted the first salmon caught each season, for they were thought to be leaders, capable of influencing all who followed. The wife of a Kwakiutl fisherman, for example, said a special prayer to the first salmon caught by her husband before she cut into the catch: "Thank you, Swimmers, you Supernatural Ones, that you have come to save our lives, mine and my husband's, that we may not die of hunger, you Long Life Maker." The woman ended her prayer by urging the salmon to return, "that we may meet again next year."

Besides performing such rituals, women routinely cleaned and preserved the huge catches of salmon and other fish provided by the men of their household. In some places, fish could be dried for storage after cleaning simply by hanging the strips on racks in the sun. This technique worked best at sites well inland from the coast, where persistent sunshine and dry winds could preserve a fresh catch of salmon within a matter of days. In many spots, however, damp weather made it essential to smoke the fish before it spoiled. Most fishing camps were equipped with at least one smokehouse, built of cedar planks, where women kept a fire smoldering night and day. Even fish heads were preserved there, to be used later for stews. Protracted smoking removed all moisture from the fish and left it tough and durable. Women placed the pieces in boxes and stored them in earthen cellars, or strung them from lines in their houses. When it came time to eat the dried chunks, they could be steamed and dipped in eulachon oil to make them more palatable.

The flesh of fur-bearing animals played a much smaller part in the diet of the coastal peoples. Nonetheless, the stalking of bear, deer, moun-

GIVING THANKS TO THE SALMON

Determined to preserve aspects of their culture, the Haida of the Queen Charlotte Islands—which they call by the ancient name of Haida Gwaii—have clung to a number of their time-honored customs, including the ritualized harvesting of the bounty of the nearby sea. One of the high points of the Haida year, in fact, remains the season in May and June during which the salmon, the most prized of all fish, leave the ocean and make their runs up the island rivers on their way to spawn. Just as their ancestors did in ages past, Haida families today travel to fishing camps to catch and preserve salmon in the traditional ways.

In recent years, the people of Haida

The Davidson family's fishing camp (top) nestles on the banks of the salmon-rich Yakoun River. Above, Claude Davidson, the family patriarch, guides his outboard-powered boat, a pair of sockeye salmon on board, up the river toward the camp.

Gwaii have also seen a rebirth of the kind of joyous rituals that were held long ago to celebrate the year's catch. In 1988 the first salmon celebration to be held in many generations of Haidas took place on the banks of the Yakoun River, off Massett Inlet. The following year, a prominent Haida family, the Davidsons—whose fishing camp, with its smokehouse and other buildings constructed by family members, is shown here and on the next two pages—staged another seasonal festival to honor the salmon and give thanks for its bounty. It was the kind of occasion, full of singing, dancing, and feasting, that has helped renew and reassert the Haida's cultural identity and pride.

Working at a big table at the camp, Claude Davidson (left) cleans silvery, freshly caught salmon by gutting them and cutting off the heads. After that, he will fillet the salmon (inset), making the thinnest possible slices using a handmade slicing knife. In the past, such slicing was done by women using knives that were made from mussel shells.

Carefully arranged on a special rack, fillets of salmon dry in the sun by the banks of the river, which has been strung with nets and floats. After a day in the sun, the fillets will be hung in the Davidsons' smokehouse (inset) to be further cured with the smoke of alder wood.

Haida chief of the village of Dadens, Claude Davidson, dressed in the attire of his office with an ermine-trimmed headpiece (right), sings a prayer song at the 1989 celebration of the salmon harvest. The festival was hosted by his son Robert, seen above singing a Haida song while beating a drum.

John Davidson, nephew of Claude, whirls and stomps as he leads others in a traditional Haida dance. He is wearing a handsome frontlet, leggings painted with images of frogs, and a breechcloth decorated with rattles made of deer hoofs.

Sara Florence Davidson, Robert's daughter (below), serves up plates of food at the festival, which included a sit-down dinner for 500 people. In addition to salmon, the feast included other products of Haida Gwaii: halibut, crab, and venison.

tain goats, seals, sea otters, and other elusive quarry was a pursuit that brought honor to the men—and a dividend to their households in the form of useful pelts. The hides were especially important in the north, where they provided extra protection against the winter cold. To the south, where freezing temperatures were rare, clothing was sparse. There men sometimes went bare, while women wore skirts woven of shredded cedar bark—the region's essential fabric; in rainy weather, both sexes put on capes and hats made of that same material, although chiefs sometimes donned fur robes. To the north, however, outfits were more substantial. Tlingit women, reported one European explorer in 1779, favored ''a long robe of smooth skin, girded about the loins, and not unlike that of our monks, covering them from the neck to the feet, and with sleeves reaching down to the wrists.'' The men, for their part, customarily wore breechcloths and fur cloaks—and some of them even put on hide shirts and leggings.

To obtain furs, men set snares or deadfall traps, or stalked their quarry either with bows and arrows or with long spears tipped with barbs of bone. Some groups employed a whip sling, or atlatl, to propel darts whose feathers made a whistling sound as they shot through the air toward the prey. Sea mammals were killed with wooden lances or harpoons, equipped with detachable stone heads that made it possible for the long, carefully crafted shafts to be used time and again. Throwing a harpoon with power and precision required great skill, and only chiefs were afforded the honor. Hunters pursued sea mammals in narrow canoes, their hulls scorched and sanded down to a sleek smoothness to enable them to skim through the water quickly and quietly.

Among northern peoples, including the Tlingit and the Tsimshian, a favorite prey of hunters was the mountain goat, whose hair was woven into splendid ornamental blankets that could be worn, displayed, or given away at potlatches. Coastal peoples to the south sometimes used dog fur for the same purpose, but

Basket slung from her shoulder, a Kwakiutl woman picks salmonberries in this photograph that was taken in the early 20th century. The women of the Northwest Coast gathered these salmon-colored raspberries and other fruits to supplement the seafood and meat provided by their male relatives.

LEGACY OF THE RAVEN

Light but tough, this spruce-root basket was used by a Klallam woman from Puget Sound to carry heavy loads such as clams. Its open weave meant that an entire load of mollusks could be rinsed by simply dunking the filled basket into water. Its adjustable strap, including the colorfully embroidered forehead band, was woven from hemp.

greater prestige was attached to the so-called Chilkat blankets, named after a northern Tlingit tribe whose men were among the most prolific hunters of the mountain goat. To corner goats and other quarry, the Tlingit bred special hunting dogs, including a terrier-like breed that nipped at the heels of bears and kept them at bay until the hunters arrived and dispatched the prey. Hunters ritually prepared young bear dogs to sniff out their prey by cutting the pup's nose and rubbing it with the fur or entrails of a bear. Tlingit hunters were fond of their dogs, and as a result, the canines proliferated. A visitor to the native village at Wrangell during the 19th century noted that "there was surely a dog apiece to every member of the community, and then, perhaps, some to spare." By that time, domestic cats had been introduced to the region by whites. Unlike the dogs, however, the cats "were kept ignominiously tied by short ropes," to keep them from stealing the dried fish that hung about the houses.

For the Tlingit as for other coastal groups, the sheer variety of natural resources available to them produced a busy and exhilarating seasonal round. "In spring, the Tlingit on the mainland coast hunt and trap bear, marten, and mink," reported George Emmons, an American naval officer who lived for many years among the Tlingit in the late 1800s and documented their customs. "Those on the island shores hunt fur seals in April and May. They also catch and dry halibut in April and May, and gather herring spawn." In the early spring as well, men would hunt sea otters from their canoes. But when the salmon appeared, Emmons noted, the Tlingit would "devote themselves wholly to this industry as long as the fish run." The chinook spawned first, followed by smaller species, with runs continuing into September. Then the Tlingit would dig for roots and tubers—including potatoes, introduced by Europeans in the late 18th century. Fall was also the time for men to hunt mountain goats and prowl once more for bear, when the animals were fattest. By the middle of October, most people were back from their hunting and fishing camps and were settling into their winter villages for the cold, dark months ahead.

All along the Northwest Coast, the return to the permanent villages from the various camps marked a welcome transition from the time of gathering to the time of expending. As a consequence of Nature's gener-

As her daughter watches, a Bella Coola woman threads eulachon onto a stick. These tiny smelt will be hung from a rack and allowed to dry in the sun. Although the fish were prized mainly for their oil, a popular condiment, a portion of the spring catch was dried and eaten during the winter.

osity, most people not only lived free from want but also had the leisure to enrich their lives through artistry and ceremony. From the simple gifts of flesh and fiber came a village life of great complexity and elegance.

Dependent as they were on the sea and its creatures, most coastal peoples constructed their villages either on sheltered ocean harbors or along rivers or estuaries that lay close to the sea. Such settlements, which might have as few as 50 inhabitants or as many as several hundred, consisted of one or two rows of houses and other structures—smokehouses, sweat lodges, storage sheds, and special seclusion huts for women during menstruation and childbirth—built parallel to the shore. The largest of the villages sometimes stretched for a mile or more along the shoreline. All the buildings were framed of wood, usually durable planks of red cedar, which aged to a silvery gray.

People lived in these communities throughout the winter months, and often returned there during the summer between their foraging expeditions. Some groups—including the Coast Salish, the Nootka, and the Bella Coola (Nuxalk), a Salishan-speaking group who lived south of the Tsimshian—carried their shelters with them when they ventured off by stripping the winter houses of their wall planks and transporting them lashed between their canoes to summer camps, where the planks were used to cover temporary shelters. Later, the process was reversed, and the planks were brought back to the coastal villages and reattached to their original posts and beams. So thoroughly did these villagers disassemble their winter houses that early European explorers who happened upon them during the summer months often concluded that the skeleton structures were the ruins of abandoned settlements.

The primary political and social unit among the coastal peoples was not the village but the household, which consisted of up to a dozen or more related families. Like the noble houses of medieval Europe, each Northwest Coast household had its own heraldry, territory, rights, and property—including the large building that served as the collective residence. These structures were sometimes magnificently decorated, inside and out, with elaborate emblems and crests. Most were given names that reflected the family's crest, such as Killer Whale House, and those names remained with the structures no matter how many times they were torn down and rebuilt on the same site.

The construction of a house was instigated by the household chief. George Emmons noted that every Tlingit chief aspired "to build or rebuild a house, and to this end he saved throughout his life; and if he died before being able to accomplish this, it was a solemn obligation to be carried out by his successor." House building was a long and formal process, requiring a variety of feasts and ceremonies. The Tlingit, for example, held a ritual called Feeding the Trees after the heavy timbers for the house's corner posts, crossbeams, and totem pole had been felled in the forest. During the ceremony, offerings of food were cast into a fire to honor the trees, which were believed to possess spirits. The Kwakiutl conducted similar rituals to honor what they called the *nawalak,* or "soul," of the living wood. The timbers often came from a special stand of cedar trees that belonged to the chief through either inheritance or purchase. Cut quickly but carefully with large mussel-shell blades or adzes made of stone, they were hauled to the nearest navigable waterway and towed behind canoes to the village. Among the Tlingit, the paddlers conveying the cedar posts "sang to the accompaniment of a drum as they approached the village," Emmons recounted, while "two or more headmen in ceremonial dress danced in the stern of the canoe."

After the rituals had been performed and the corner posts set in place, the builders added the heavy interlocking framework of interior posts and crossbeams. Then they secured the floor, roof, and wall planks with cedar-bark withes or wooden pegs that served in place of nails. Heavy stones were placed on the roof planks in order to keep them from blowing off in strong winds.

The configuration of the house varied from place to place. The northern groups built large houses with gable roofs, generally about 40 feet square, and each contained a huge central hearth. Although many of these structures had a hidden tunnel for use by the chief and his close kin during ceremonies, or as an escape route during an enemy raid, the only visible opening was the smoke hole in the roof—which could be covered in rainy weather with a sliding mat—and a small rectangular or oval doorway in the side of the house that faced the beach. The members of some households painted or carved a crest design around the doorway so that the gaping mouth of the crest figure formed the entrance.

Farther south, among the Coast Salish and other groups, many of the houses were constructed with shed roofs and multiple hearths, one for each family unit. Coast Salish houses were sometimes built end to end, with doorways in between, forming a continuous structure large enough to house an entire village. In 1808 explorer Simon Fraser described one such edifice—a prodigy measuring 60 feet wide and 650 feet long.

Members of a Kwakiutl family are dwarfed
by the interior house posts of a winter lodge
under construction on Gilford Island, British Columbia. Ceremoniously carved from
the trunks of cedar trees, the posts depict
the family's mythical ancestors. Once completed, the house will be revered as a living
entity and will be given a proper name.

The characteristic, freestanding house along the Northwest Coast had a central communal space that was used for ceremonies, games, and chores. Around the perimeter of the room was a wide wooden platform, covered with cedar-bark sleeping mats or fur blankets and partitioned into cubicles by means of screens or piles of boxes and baskets. John Jewitt, an English-born sailor who was taken captive by the Nootka in the early 1800s and lived with them for two years, noted that their furnishings consisted only of "boxes, in which they put their clothes, furs, and such things as they hold most valuable; tubs for keeping their provisions of spawn and blubber in; trays from which they eat; baskets for their dried fish and other purposes; and bags made of bark matting, of which they also make their beds." The cubicles served as the living quarters of the individual families and were allotted according to rank. The house chief and his immediate family occupied the place of honor, usually the far wall opposite the door. The families ranked right below the chief lived adjacent to his cubicle, with the families ranked lower still occupying the cubicles next to them, and so on around the room. Those at the bottom of the social ladder—the slaves—occupied the area next to the door, where they were vulnerable to both cold winter drafts and surprise attacks.

Slaves were obtained primarily through raids led by the chief or a principal warrior. There were many motives for going to war, including thirst for booty, the need to atone for the loss of a relative by capturing or killing an enemy—whether or not that enemy was directly responsible for the loss—or the desire to repay some nonlethal insult that had brought dishonor to the household. Sometimes blood feuds between kinship groups spread so that whole villages became involved, but most attacks were aimed at the occupants of a specific house. Warriors typically crept up on the house late at night and forced their way in, claiming lives or carrying off prisoners before the startled residents could mount a defense. During such raids, the Nootka and other groups sometimes took the heads of their victims as trophies.

Among the Kwakiutl, elders prepared boys for combat by encouraging them to lash out at one another with nettles and twigs or to engage in other violent contests. Charley Nowell, a high-ranking Kwakiutl born in 1870, described a diverting war game that he and his companions played: "We don't

Sculpted in the form of a beaver, this alder bowl made by a Makah artisan once held a fish oil condiment at potlatches, elaborate gift-giving celebrations. The bowl was also a family emblem that reminded potlatch guests of their host's affluence.

Three crest figures— an eagle, raven, and a bearlike human— cling to the handle of this Haida spoon. Such ornate items were used for formal occasions.

use any weapons," he said; "we just fight with our bare hands to go and get slaves." To win slaves, the opposing teams ran at each other head-on and tried to pick up their opponents and carry them off. Afterward, the two sides exchanged their captives, one for one, until the stronger team was left with a surplus of slaves and claimed victory.

The game was not too far removed from the reality of warfare in earlier times. Captives taken as the result of feuds between houses might be killed, but many nobles were kept alive and later ransomed by their relatives, who offered property for their release. The ransomed individual would then undergo some form of ritual cleansing before rejoining society. Less fortunate were the captives taken during long-distance raids carried out expressly to seize slaves. Such people could have little hope of ever regaining their freedom; even if a freeman married a slave, any child she bore would remain a slave, with rare exceptions.

This colorful basket was crafted from cedar roots, bear grass, and cherry bark by a Coast Salish woman. Practical as well as beautiful, baskets were used by the Coast Salish for everything from infant cradles to berry containers.

Although slaves had no status within the community and little chance of ever obtaining any, their living conditions were not much different from those of their owners. "They reside in the same house, forming as it were a part of the family, are usually kindly treated, eat of the same food, and live as well as their masters," noted John Jewitt. He added that slaves "are compelled however at times to labour severely, as not only all the menial offices are performed by them, such as bringing water, cutting wood, and a variety of others, but they are obliged to make the canoes, to assist in building and repairing the houses, to supply their masters with fish, and to attend them to war and to fight for them."

Slaves whose proven skills endeared them to their masters might eventually be freed. But those who had been recently acquired had reason to fear for their lives. When building an important new house, for example, nobles sometimes sacrificed several slaves obtained specifically for that purpose; the bodies were placed beneath the corner posts. When a great chief died, one or more slaves would be slain to assist him in the afterlife. Young slaves were sometimes designated to serve as companions to a newborn child—and to accompany the child to the spirit world in the event of its death. Explorer Samuel Parker told of an incident that occurred in 1829, when the wife of an influential Chinook chief ordered two female slaves sacrificed after her young daughter died so that they

could watch over the child eternally. Valued slaves who became ill were nursed back to health, but those who were too old or infirm to be of further use might be left in the woods to perish.

Ranked above the slaves in the social hierarchy were the commoners and the nobility. The nobility consisted of chiefs and their close relatives, who often served the community in prestigious positions—as shamans, for example, or as warriors. The commoners were those who had only distant ties to a chief. They customarily had to do their own menial labor, although some were fortunate enough, through raiding or trading, to obtain slaves for that purpose. Commoners were also expected to give reg-

At Wrangell, Alaska, in 1898, a combination of Western and Indian creature comforts fills the cedar-plank home of a Tlingit chief named Lot. Despite the introduction of iron cookware and modern dishes, Northwest Indians continued to use wooden crest bowls like the one at right at feasts and celebrations. Such gatherings were frequently held at the chief's lodge, which was large enough to double as a public hall.

ular gifts of tribute—the first meat of a hunt, for example—to the nobles.

The distinction between the two classes was particularly well wrought among the northern peoples. The Tlingit, for example, referred to those of high rank as "noble" or "good," while commoners were called "poor children," or "just anything." The nobles seldom performed lowly tasks such as fetching firewood or water, and usually they wore fancier clothes and finer ornaments than the commoners. In addition to their material advantages, the nobles inherited a diverse array of privileges, such as the right to perform certain dances at ceremonial functions, or to tattoo a particular family crest on their bodies, or to pass on certain names of honor to their children. They also had the right—and the responsibility—to give potlatches and to marry within their rank. Marrying beneath one's inherited rank could bring social disaster. As late as 1885, a Tlingit chief named Brown Bear lost social standing when he married a woman considered to be a commoner. Two chiefs from other Tlingit groups refused to attend the marriage ceremony, saying that "no good could come of mating a chief with a clam digger."

Farther south, the division between nobles and commoners was somewhat less distinct. The Kwakiutl evolved fine gradations of rank, and it was not easy to discern whether those at the middle levels were low-ranking noblemen or high-ranking commoners. Here, as among the Coast Salish, social advancement was possible. A commoner who demonstrated great skill as a canoe builder, for example, might be rewarded by his chief with privileges. The ability to gain wealth through trade or warfare might also enable a commoner to sponsor a small potlatch and thereby lay claim to a title. The phenomenon of potlatching one's way up the social ladder grew prevalent among the Kwakiutl after European-kindled epidemics ravaged the population in the mid-1800s and created hundreds of openings in the hierarchy, even as new trading posts in the territory provided opportunities to acquire wealth. In the central and southern regions, one peculiar way of accruing wealth and stature in many communities was to succeed at gambling. Like other Native Americans, the peoples of the Northwest Coast esteemed winners in games of chance not only for their skill but also for their spiritual endowment, since good fortune was thought to be a gift from unseen powers. One gambling game, played with variations all along the coast, called for a contestant to look on as his opponent shifted two small objects such as carved pieces of bone—one marked and the other plain—back and forth between his hands. Sometimes the man with the bones would toss the pieces in the air, or transfer them behind his back. All the while, teammates lined up on either side of the two players would make wagers, beat sticks, and sing songs. In the end, the contestant would have to guess in which hand his opponent was hiding the unmarked piece. Among the Tlingit, the two players were supposed to stare into each other's eyes throughout the contest, which meant that the outcome depended largely on the ability of the guesser to read the expressions of his opponent.

However such games were played, winning on a regular basis was difficult, and anyone who did so was honored and rewarded. The Chinook told a story of a young commoner who rose quickly into the upper class as a result of his phenomenal success at gambling. "That lousy boy made everybody poor," one storyteller marveled. Despite their disdain for the boy's humble origins, the Chinook nobility permitted him entry into their ranks, for they believed he had acquired an especially powerful guardian spirit.

Her labret, or lip plug, marking her as a woman of wealth, a Tlingit mother proudly shows off her baby in this 18th-century color sketch. The child wears another symbol of the family's status, a nose ornament.

The heads of the various households exercised leadership among the coastal peoples. Such chiefs were usually men, although some women oversaw households, particularly among the Coast Salish. The chief's re-

Carved in the shape of an eagle's head and inlaid with abalone shell, this wooden labret (top) fit inside a slit cut into a Tlingit woman's lower lip. A nose ornament (bottom) fashioned from abalone shell and incised with a killer-whale design was suspended from the septum of a Kwakiutl woman.

sponsibilities and rights varied. Among the Tsimshian, chiefs set aside food and other supplies to ensure that their kin would have enough to make it through the year. Although they received regular tribute and thus had little need to forage for themselves, many Tsimshian chiefs chose to participate in the hunting of sea lions and mountain goats, both to prove their courage and endurance and to show that they were in touch with the powers that brought success in hunting. Among the Nootka, whale hunting was exclusively the sport of chiefs and their close kin.

Within a given village, one household always took precedence over the others, and its leader was recognized as the chief of that community. But his authority was limited. Any decisions he reached had to be approved by the heads of other households. With their assent, he might undertake a communal project, perhaps pooling the resources of the village to build a new fishing weir.

Such political bonds were weak, however, compared with the force of the clan ties that linked one household to another. Within a large Tlingit village, there would be several households belonging to different clans. The clan was an extension of one's household, and people were expected to support and defend their fellow clan members much as they would their own housemates. If their help was requested, for example, the men of one household might join nearby clansmen on a raid. And an entire household frequently made contributions in advance to a potlatch given by their clan relatives.

Each Tlingit clan belonged, in turn, to one of two larger groups—designated by crests as the Ravens or the Wolves— whose members were expected to perform important services for their opposite numbers. When a chief among the Ravens decided to build a new house, he would put on his poorest clothes and supplicate chiefs among the Wolves, whose people would then build the house in exchange for food and other gifts. The most important connection between Wolves and Ravens, however, was that a member of one group was required to choose a mate from the other group. Every marriage was a

PRESTIGIOUS HEADGEAR

Generations of Northwest Coast Indians have displayed their totems on various surfaces, including houses, blankets, and weapons. Among the most valued of all such totems is the clan crest hat. Carved, usually of cedar, or woven of spruce root and decorated with the image of an animal or supernatural being associated with the clan, the headpiece appeared only at potlatches and other important events. While wearing the hat, a chief distributed lavish gifts to other clans in order to protect the claim to the crest. Although hats in theory belonged to the entire clan, certain leaders, such as this Chilkat couple *(opposite),* acted as trustees. The man holds a killer-whale hat; his wife shows the murrelet. Behind them sits a bear hat with seven woven rings.

TLINGIT WOLF

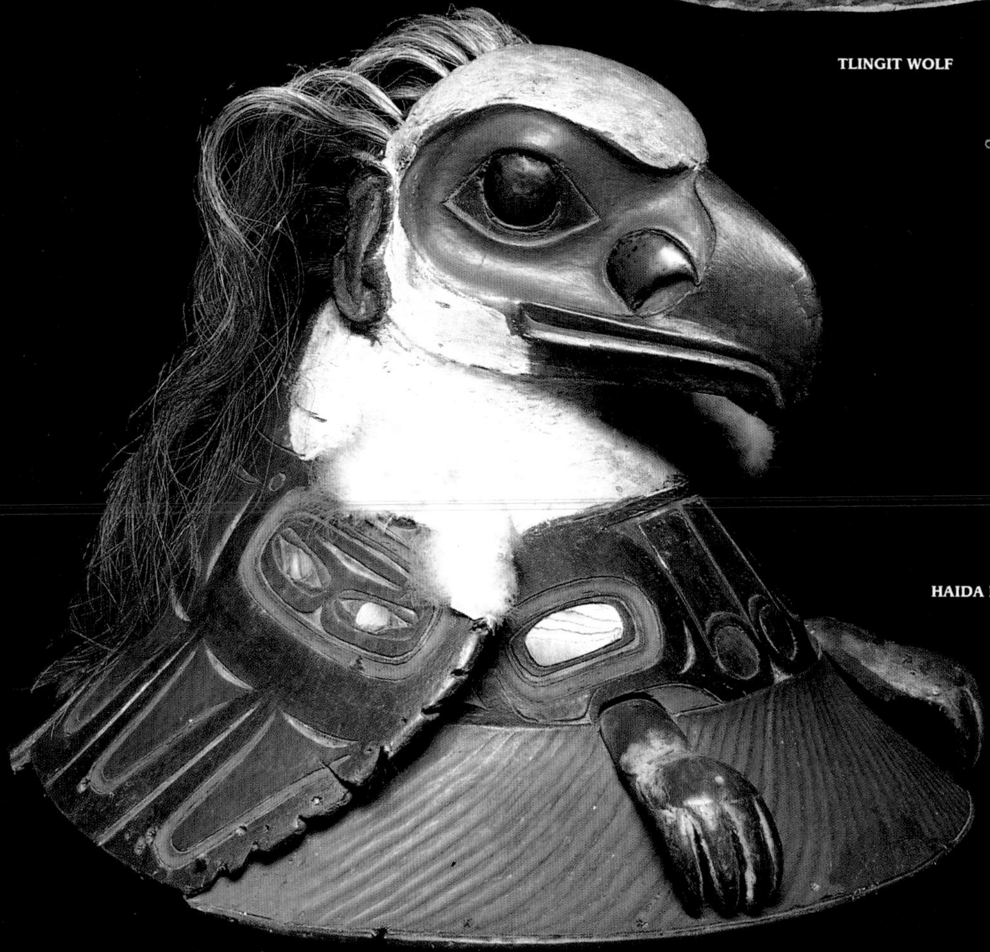

HAIDA EAGLE

HAIDA BEAVER

TLINGIT RAVEN

Regally outfitted in a Chilkat blanket and leggings, and holding a raven rattle similar to the one above, a Tlingit chief sits for the camera. The rattle shows the trickster Raven flying off with a red sun clasped in its beak. On his back is a tableau of a raven lending power to a man through its beak.

union of a Wolf with a Raven, and the effect was to knit Tlingit society together. Children inherited their affiliation from their mother, so that a boy whose father was a Wolf and whose mother was a Raven became a Raven himself. To reinforce that affiliation, he would be sent at an early age to live with his mother's brother, in a household dominated by Raven men. The boy would remain on affectionate terms with his natural father and other Wolves, but his maternal uncle raised him under the Raven crest. The boy's sister, for her part, would remain with her mother and father through puberty, after which she would marry a Wolf and go to live with him in his household, while maintaining her identity as a Raven and bequeathing it to her children.

The Tsimshian and Haida organized themselves along similar lines, with affiliation passing from mother to child. Here, as among the Tlingit, a boy who went to live with his maternal uncle had much to learn about the customs and lore associated with the household, the clan, and the crest. A young nobleman, in particular, had many sacred stories to memorize, tales bequeathed by his ancestors. After reaching a certain age, he was expected to recount those stories, word for word. To forget the words was to neglect one's inheritance.

Among the Kwakiutl, Nootka, and Bella Coola, a son or daughter could choose the affiliation of either parent. In place of clans, the Kwakiutl had groups they called *numaym,* or "those of one kind," whose members traced their descent to a common supernatural ancestor. Each numaym had a fixed number of titles that determined the rank of the various nobles. These titles were known as "seats" or "standing places" because

Only members of the nobility were permitted to display crests such as the raven head jutting from the home of a Kwakiutl chief in this 1915 photograph. A painting on the front of the house repeats the raven motif; figures representing other crests belonging to the chief's family were erected nearby.

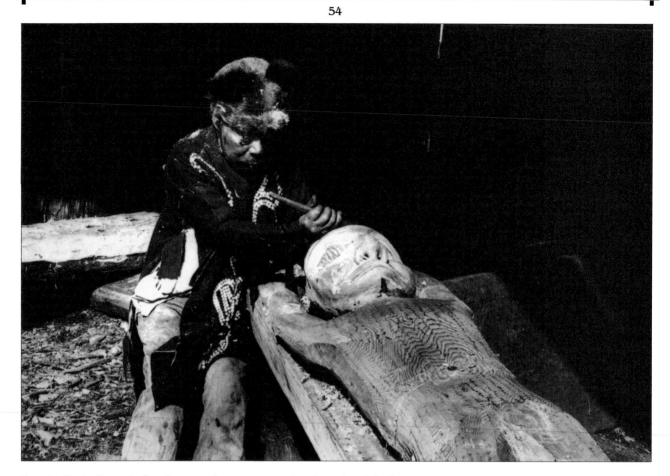

they indicated precisely where each person was to sit or stand during pot-latches and other ceremonies. According to Kwakiutl legend, the seats had been given to the people by animal spirits at the beginning of the world, when these humanlike creatures were still all-powerful.

In general, Kwakiutl titles were passed on to sons, although parents without male heirs might confer a title on their daughter, whose husband would then hold it in trust for his own son. When a privileged youngster came of age, he would claim an ancestral title—a name of honor and the crests, privileges, and property that went along with it—from the nu-maym of his father or mother at a potlatch sponsored by his household. The purpose of the gift giving was to validate the youngster's claim to the title, for only those who could confer bounty on others were worthy of a seat. If an ancestral title was not passed along to a descendant in this way, it might be claimed by an outsider and lost to the family forever. After contact with whites, when epidemics left some Kwakiutl parents without heirs, they sometimes conferred an important title on a familiar object, such as a house post, and staged a mock marriage in which that object was given away to a suitable bridegroom, whose son would then inherit the title and preserve the family legacy.

Farther south, among the Coast Salish and Chinook, social organiza-tion was less structured. By and large, an individual's status had less to do with inheritance than with demonstrated talent. And young people

Wearing a button blanket and a cap fash-ioned from a bear's head, a Tlingit carver carefully adds a human figure to a totem pole. Because such work was viewed as sa-cred, it could be done only by carvers who were recognized as master craftsmen.

were bound by fewer conventions. Married couples had the freedom to reside with either of their in-laws. Although about two-thirds of the couples chose to move in with the husband's family, those who set up residence with the wife's parents did not suffer loss of status because of it. Nor were such decisions always permanent: Families could come and go freely between the houses of their parents.

For the most part, however, the coastal peoples observed strict protocol in their social lives and attached tremendous importance to a person's ancestry. Pride in one's forebears was not simply a question of vanity. Ultimately it was a sacred matter, for families traced their origins to encounters with spirits and could tell of many instances in which supernatural powers had come to the aid of their ancestors and strengthened the lineage. Such guiding spirits were portrayed on many of the objects people used and admired in their daily lives, ranging from utilitarian items such as canoes, storage boxes, tools, weapons, and blankets to ceremonial artifacts such as the great wooden screens arrayed in front of the chief's cubicle during potlatches and other rituals. "The taste of ornament prevails in all the works of their hands," observed Captain Étienne Marchand, a French mariner who visited the Northwest Coast in 1792. "Their canoes, their chests, and different little articles of furniture in use among them, are covered with figures that might be taken for a species of hieroglyphics," he added. "Fishes and other animals, heads of men, and various whimsical designs, are mingled and confounded in order to compose a subject."

The mingled "hieroglyphic" figures described by Marchand were in fact crest designs—stylized representations of the spiritual patrons of a particular family, some of whom appeared as animals and others as humans, hybrids, or natural phenomena such as the sun and moon. Like European coats of arms, Northwest Coast crest figures proclaimed the importance of the household that owned them. But more than that, they embodied the sacred history of the family. At potlatches and other ceremonies, the story connected to each crest symbol would be told and retold—how a spirit befriended and sustained the first ancestors, for example, or how members of a later generation journeyed to the family's current home, enduring fearful trials inflicted by tricksters or monsters before protective powers intervened to save them. Thus the crest figures constituted an expression of the family's unique her-

This totem pole, which measures just over six feet tall, is a large model of a life-size one that stood before the home of the Haida chief Skulka in the late 19th century. The pole features a Russian officer, who appears near the top sporting a beard and epaulets. Above him is an eagle; immediately below him is a thunderbird, and at bottom, a bear that is biting a small round-eyed creature.

itage as well as a way of transmitting that tradition to future generations.

For this reason, crest designs have always been carefully guarded by the families that own them. Disputes over the right to crests were sometimes resolved through battle in the old days and through intense if bloodless competitions in more recent times. An ethnographer who lived among the Haida in the early 1900s observed that "if any chief learned that one of his crests had been adopted by a chief of a family that was considered of lower rank, he would put the latter to shame, and by giving away or destroying more property than the other chief could muster, force him to abandon it." In one such case, a Haida chief whose family claimed exclusive right to the mountain goat crest discovered that a rival family of less wealth and stature had adopted the same crest. He shamed the pretenders into relinquishing use of that crest by staging a potlatch his rivals could never hope to equal. To be sure, crests did switch hands from time to time. They were sometimes captured in war, for example, or offered as compensation for murder. To avoid the humiliation of seeing their crests displayed by another lineage, however, a family often went to great expense to buy them back and ceremonially redeem them.

The supreme expression of a family's devotion to its spiritual heritage was the totem pole. Usually carved of cedar, these exquisitely sculpted columns varied in size and style according to their function. There was the giant, freestanding memorial pole erected in honor of a chief who had died; the mortuary pole, with a cavity at the top to hold the cremated remains of a chief or other noble; the frontal pole that framed the entryway of some houses to proclaim the identity, worth, and status of the family to all those entering their dwelling; and the interior post that served as a support for the crossbeam while detailing the owners' proud pedigree.

With their sundry figures arrayed one atop the other, totem poles celebrated the many forces that contrived to make a house great—spirits associated not only with the immediate household but also with the clan or crest to which the household belonged. Prominent among the totems carved by the coastal peoples were familiar creatures, including Killer Whale, Wolf, Raven, and Eagle—and mythical raptors such as Thunderbird and the bird-monster Hokhokw, who could split a man's skull open with his long beak. Families gratefully acknowledged the patronage of these spirits, for they knew that prosperity came only through struggle. Thus they honored the powers of cunning and rapacity no less than they did the spirit of generosity epitomized by the salmon and other gracious beings who gave freely of themselves each year. ✠

In this reenactment, costumed dancers perform in exquisite canoes carrying a wealthy Kwakiutl groom and his wedding party to the village of his future wife. Because by custom an individual married only a person of equal rank who belonged to another clan, prominent men often had to travel far to find a mate. Such unions served as political alliances and were sealed by an exchange of crests and other family property.

A face representing the guiding spirit of a sea lion is portrayed on the animal's flipper in a detail from the Black Skin Post (opposite), which graced the interior of the Whale House. The post shows the mythical clan hero Dukt'oohl ripping the sea lion in two. Before he revealed his strength, Dukt'oohl was mockingly called "Black Skin" for sleeping late by the smoky house fire.

LEGACY OF THE WHALE HOUSE

In the early 1800s, a wealthy and influential Tlingit chief named Xetsuwu decided to build a great house with the help of his clan, the powerful Gaanax-teidi. He spared no expense to make it the most impressive structure in his home village of Kluk-wan, on Alaska's Chilkat River. Called the Whale House after a crest long associated with the clan, the building, framed of spruce planks, was unadorned on the outside. But inside it was embellished with some of the finest carvings in the Pacific Northwest. Much of the work was done by a master carver named Kadjisdoo'akch, recruited by Xetsuwu from distant Kasitlaan—near present-day Wrangell—to lend the Whale House a majesty that only an artist with the talent to bring powerful spirits to life could confer.

For the Whale House, Kadjisdoo'akch sculpted such treasures as a 14-foot-long ceremonial bowl and the house post shown here—one of four interior columns he carved with interwoven human and animal figures depicting clan legends. He was paid a princely fee: 10 slaves, 50 dressed moose skins, and many blankets. Xetsuwu must have been well pleased. The Whale House stood for about 80 years as a tribute to the prestige of his clan. In time, the structure deteriorated beyond repair, but the great carvings survived and are acknowledged today as supreme expressions of the native woodworker's craft.

The aging Whale House—shown above about 1895—was torn down in 1899 by then-clan leader Yeilgooxu (standing at near left beside another prominent clan member). New structures were later built in Klukwan in order to perpetuate the name of the house and to hold its treasures.

A multifamily residence as well as a ceremonial center, the Whale House measured nearly 50 feet wide by 53 feet long. The four carved interior house posts, each more than 9 feet tall and 2.5 feet wide, supported massive roof beams. The plank floor was recessed at the center to provide a cooking area around the central fire. Residents slept on the surrounding platform at night. Each family was assigned a place according to its social standing. Lower-ranking inhabitants occupied the front of the house; higher-ranking individuals claimed the back. The rearmost area, behind a wooden screen—carved separately by an anonymous artist—known as the Rain Wall, was reserved for the household leader, or "hit'saati."

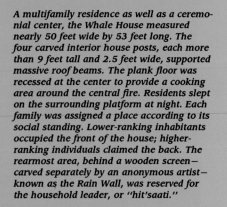

WOODWORM POST

RAIN WALL

FIRST PLATFORM

LOWER FLOOR

FIREPLACE

BLACK SKIN POST

RAVEN POST

SMOKE HOLE

UPPER PLATFORM

SEA CREATURE POST

ENTRY

Animal and human attributes are melded in the Sea Creature Post, which shows the legendary figure Gunakadeit clenching a whale's tail between his teeth. In Tlingit legend, a young man of the Yakutat region caught the sea monster, donned his skin, and assumed the powers of Gunakadeit—a creature strong enough to seize whales and carry them home to feed his kin. Portrayed within the whale's tail is a Yakutat woman (detail, opposite). Perched atop Gunakadeit's head, a hawk between her hands, is his child, one of the Daughters of the Creek responsible for summoning salmon upstream to spawn.

The Woodworm Post portrays a fabled
Gaanaxteidi Clan member, Kaakutchaan
(top), embracing the woodworm she adopted during her confinement at puberty and
nursed like a baby until it grew huge and
began crawling out at night to eat food
stored in her village. Soon her parents discovered the monster and had it killed. The
girl died of grief, and her remorseful relatives took the woodworm as a crest. The
post represents the tree in which the woodworm lived—the crane at the base (detail,
upper right) stands for the branches, and
the frog in its bill symbolizes the roots.

The central figure of
the Rain Wall repre-
sents Raven, with
clawlike feet and
human arms out-
stretched from the
opening that serves
as the entrance to
the house leader's
chamber. The small,
crouching figures
bordering the screen
symbolize raindrops
sent by Raven.

The great clan feast dish was carved in the shape of a giant woodworm, portrayed with human features at either end to signify the close ancestral bond between the clan and the crest animal.

The chest belonging to the Whale House leader held such items as clan regalia and emblems of rank, including dancing blankets, headdresses, and heraldic images. A chief frequently used his chest as a seat on ceremonial occasions; upon his death, it held his cremated remains.

The Raven Post features a humanlike configuration of Raven, shown with Raven as a bird (detail, above) flying from his mouth and with his feet resting on a king salmon he has seized. He grasps a lifelike figure he has used to lure his prey. According to clan legend, Raven fooled the king salmon by telling the fish of insults the figure had supposedly uttered: "He says that you have an ugly black mouth and that you are afraid to come up to the shore." Goaded, the salmon swam to shore and jumped into a tidal pool, where he became food for Raven.

In an 1895 photograph taken of the original Whale House, clan members display their riches against the backdrop of the Rain Wall; the Woodworm Dish is at the base of the wall, flanked by the Woodworm Post (left) and the Raven Post. Brought out to celebrate a potlatch, the clan treasures include moose-skin tunics, carved boxes, crest hats, guns, and a huge carved head.

THE VENERABLE POTLATCH

The potlatch, an institution among Northwest Coast tribes, endures to this day despite a concerted effort by officialdom to suppress the celebration. In 1885, at the urging of missionaries and Indian agents, the Canadian government outlawed the gift-giving ceremony primarily on the grounds that it was wasteful and retarded the social progress of the Indians. Despite the law, most groups continued to practice the rituals in secret until the bans were lifted in 1950. As one Kwakiutl chief told an outsider, the people answered to a higher authority than the Canadian government. "It is a strict law that bids us dance. It is a strict law that bids us give away our property. It is a good law."

Potlatches feature dances, songs, and sacred rites that have changed little over the centuries. Other aspects of the ceremony, however, have evolved to conform to the demands of modern life. These gatherings, which once could take as long as 12 or more years to plan and prepare, now require only about one year of advance work. And because most participants have full-time jobs, modern potlatches last only a day, rather than four days or a full week as they did in the past. Guests now arrive on motorized fishing boats instead of in cedar canoes, and receive as gifts coffee mugs, luggage, towels, and cash in addition to more traditional Indian-made artworks.

Today's potlatches may look different from those hosted 100 years ago, but the reasons for celebrating remain the same—a death, a marriage, the raising of a house pole, or the naming of a child. Highlights of two modern Kwakiutl celebrations that took place at Alert Bay in British Columbia appear on the following pages along with archival photographs of traditional feasts and regalia.

A solitary wooden figure, arm outstretched and finger pointing, stands on a beach at high tide next to a Kwakiutl village. Such carved images, including the one at right, were positioned to face the open water and welcome the potlatch guests arriving in canoes.

Wearing masks and Chilkat blankets as did their ancestors, Kwakiutl chiefs and other invited guests cruise into Alert Bay on board the "Nimpkish Producer," a modern seine fishing boat. They were attending a potlatch to celebrate the opening of the U'mista Cultural Centre on November 1, 1980.

A DANCE OF WELCOME

When delegations from 12 Kwakiutl villages gathered to commemorate the opening of the U'mista Cultural Centre in 1980, they enjoyed a traditional potlatch welcome. Dancers representing the host chiefs donned button blankets and carved frontlets with long trains of ermine skins to perform the customary Chiefs Dance, shown at left. Guests had assembled to celebrate not only the new building but also the return of ceremonial treasures that had been surrendered to the Canadian government in 1922 in order to obtain a reduced sentence for some 45 Indians arrested for violating the potlatch ban. The center, which now houses many of the returned masks and other regalia, is decorated with a traditional design taken from the 19th-century house front of an Alert Bay chief, showing a thunderbird carrying a whale *(inset)*.

A 19th-century dance headdress, similar to those still worn by dancers at Alert Bay, features a carved wooden crest animal surrounded by a band of swansdown and feathers. Splints fashioned out of whalebone are attached to the crown.

SONGS OF MOURNING

"Yesterday we had a mourning feast, with eating, mourning songs, speeches, and a song to drive away sadness," the anthropologist Franz Boas wrote of a Kwakiutl potlatch that he attended in 1930. Boas was referring to the opening phase of all potlatches, which is given over to mourning and to offering condolences to those who have lost members of their family.

Fifty-three years later at Alert Bay, some of those same songs were sung to a group of women assembled at the community's Big House, shown at left, for the opening ceremony of a potlatch given by William T. Cranmer, who had inherited the titles and rights of a tribal chief. The songs were followed by the performance of a slow Ladies Dance, which is intended "to shake off sadness and wipe away tears" so that the celebration can proceed.

Wearing hand-appliquéd button blankets, grieving women perform the Ladies Dance to open Cranmer's 1983 potlatch. Their formal cloaks are similar to an older blanket design that features a red sun on a blue background (inset).

Bob Harris, a Kwakiutl chief who hosted several potlatches that were held at Alert Bay about the year 1900, wears a dance costume fashioned of wood and cedar bark.

A wealthy 19th-century chief holding a speaker's staff stands proudly in front of a collection of gifts that he intends to give away at an Alert Bay pot-latch, including a pile of blankets and an array of bracelets (held by the man at right). Modern chiefs continue to receive speaker's staffs (inset, right) carved with images of their spiritual ancestors.

PASSING ON
THE POWER

For hundreds of years, potlatches have marked the transfer of power from one generation to the next. This tradition continued in 1983 when James Wallas *(standing, at near right)* acted as a speaker for Chief James King *(seated, next to carved staff)* in passing on the chief's property to William T. Cranmer *(center)*. Cranmer's inheritance included the title T'lakwagila (Copper Maker), the right to perform various dances and songs, and a speaker's staff. He also received a legacy cherished by Northwest Coast Indians: a shield-shaped piece of copper *(held by Wallas)* incised with the design of a bear. Because property is usually transferred through women, Cranmer's wife Denise stands at his side with a bag of cash that will be distributed to the guests.

Bob Harris demonstrates the moving jaw and flippers of a Killer Whale Dance mask in 1903 (right). A similar 19th-century mask (below) also appeared at potlatches. Dancers assumed the guise of a whale in Peace Dances following the Hamatsa performance (opposite).

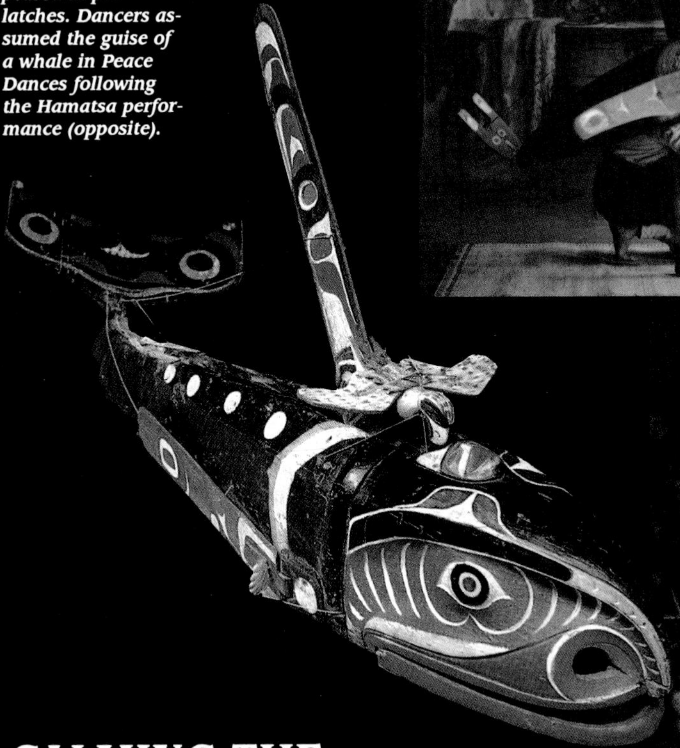

CALMING THE CANNIBAL SPIRIT

Essential to the modern potlatch are the Red Cedar Bark Dances performed by members of the Hamatsa Society, a select group whose ancestors are said to have been possessed by the supernatural Cannibal at the North End of the World. Hamatsa Dancers use whistles, elaborate headdresses, and frenzied gestures to act out the capture and calming of the Cannibal Dancer. The Cannibal Spirit is attended by masked servants, including Raven and Crooked Beak, shown performing at right. Unlike their predecessors, today's Hamatsa Dancers do not usually fast and sequester themselves in the woods to gain strength from the spirits. According to a potlatch participant, the modern dancer's vitality comes from "an intense feeling of power and belonging that is hard to describe to those who have not been part of something so vibrantly alive."

In a photograph taken about 1914, a man displays goods and gifts surrendered to the Canadian government under the potlatch ban, including masks and a Chilkat blanket. Such blankets (top) feature handwoven designs in dyed black, yellow, and white mountain goat wool, and they remain among the most treasured of all Kwakiutl family heirlooms and potlatch gifts.

DISPENSING THE BOUNTY

The word *potlatch* comes from the Chinook Jargon word for "giving," a giving that has continued on a grand scale to the present day. The Cranmers gave away thousands of dollars in cash to chiefs and singers at the end of their potlatch, shown opposite; gifts for the other guests included china, luggage, and handmade afghan blankets.

As in times past, the gifts were given as a display of the host's wealth and status, and served as a form of payment for those who bore witness to his inheritance. One of the Kwakiutls who was accused of violating the potlatch ban in 1921 explained the gift-giving tradition most eloquently: "When one's heart is glad, he gives away gifts. It was given to us by our Creator, to be our way of doing things, we who are Indians. The potlatch was given to us to be our way of expressing joy."

2

LINKS TO THE SUPERNATURAL

The bird carvings that compose this elaborate Kwakiutl mask represent the helpers of the Cannibal at the North End of the World, a supernatural creature who thrives on human flesh. The Kwakiutl use such masks during extravagantly staged dramatizations of tribal lore; such performances are central to the spiritual life of many Northwest groups.

Long ago, according to the Nootka of Vancouver Island, a chief visited his salmon trap day after day and was dismayed to find it always empty. Realizing that someone was stealing his fish, he hid in the bushes and kept watch. At length, a *winatshisht,* or "supernatural canoe," approached with a crew of 10 *ya'ai,* manlike spirits with hairy bodies and feathered ears. The chief fainted from fright and did not regain consciousness until after the spirits had paddled off downstream. Summoning his courage, he resumed his vigil. The ya'ai eventually reappeared, towing a whale behind their canoe. When the spirits stopped to make camp on the far side of the river, the chief let out a ritual scream that transformed them and the whale into foam. He carefully scooped up the frothy bubbles, knowing they contained the spiritual essence of the ya'ai and the whale. With this potent substance in his possession, he confidently moved his people down to the seashore and introduced them to a new way of life—whale hunting. The Nootka thrived at their new pursuit, and none more so than the chief, who killed one or two whales every time he ventured out to sea.

The story of that ancestral encounter is but one of countless legends linking the Indians of the Pacific Northwest to the supernatural. Like Native Americans of other areas, these coastal peoples have traditionally perceived the world as populated with a host of mysterious powers that dwell amid the region's thick forests and rugged mountains, beneath the waters of its many rivers and streams, and in the skies and ocean deeps. Indeed, a sense of the sacred permeated all aspects of their lives. Long ago, the paths of spirits and humans intersected often, allowing the Indians to acquire special skills, such as the Nootka's ability to hunt whales. Some of those skills have been passed on to later generations, and new skills have been gained, since the potency of the spirits remains undiminished, even if encounters with them are less frequent today.

According to ancient belief, the spirits were also responsible for many natural phenomena—the changing of the seasons, the movement of the sun across the sky, the maintaining of the earth in a state of balance. Most of these beings were said to be human in essence, if they were visualized at all. Many took on the guise of animals, birds, or fish, although they reverted to human shape when they returned to their own lands. Others adopted the form of plants, wearing the aspect of a wet cedar tree, a particular root, or a water-saturated stump. Still others possessed extraordinary physical traits, appearing as dwarfs, giants, monsters, sea serpents, and other fantastic creatures.

In one of their legends, the Bella Coola speak of a monstrous bearlike creature called the Sniniq, with long, silky, blue-gray hair, immense talons, and eyes that reversed in their sockets and emitted piercing beams that could strike a person senseless. Afterward, the creature would place its stunned victim in a basket on its back and return to its cave, where it would feast on human flesh at its leisure. It could be killed only with a bullet that had been coated in blood.

The ranks of the spirits included a number of other nightmarish beings that preyed on humans—mountain lions, for example, that walked backward and killed with a flick of their lancelike tails, and shadowy trees that claimed the life of anyone who dared look at them. Nootka tradition relates the story of one spirit that changed into 10 different kinds of birds; humans encountering this creature died if they failed to watch the full succession of metamorphoses.

Certain malevolent spirits were said to rely on guile to ensnare their victims. The Swheswhey of the Bella Coola enticed women into the woods by making seductive noises, then killed them. River otter spirits, associated with madness, used a variant of this ploy: They assumed the form of a loved one to lure a man or woman into their realm. According to the Tsimshian, an alert person could discover the ruse before it was too late. They recount a tale about a man walking in the woods who thought he saw his wife. At the last moment, he realized that the seeming woman had short, stubby fingers and fur behind her ears. Turning his eyes away from the apparition, he fired a shot. When he looked back, a river otter lay dead on the ground.

A creature the Bella Coola call a Skamtsk was as violent as the river otter spirits were subtle. It lived in lakes and possessed an enormous mouth that sucked with incomprehensible force. The Indians tell about a time when two boys—one poor, the other a chief's son—decided to take a swim. The chief's son dived into the water first. The other boy was about to join him when he heard a loud whooshing sound, along with strange crackling. He called out to his friend, asking him if he heard the noises.

This brightly painted Haida carving depicts Thunderbird, a legendary beast whose eyes give off lightning and whose wing beats make thunder. The face on its breast symbolizes the Haida belief that all animals possess human souls and can assume human form at will.

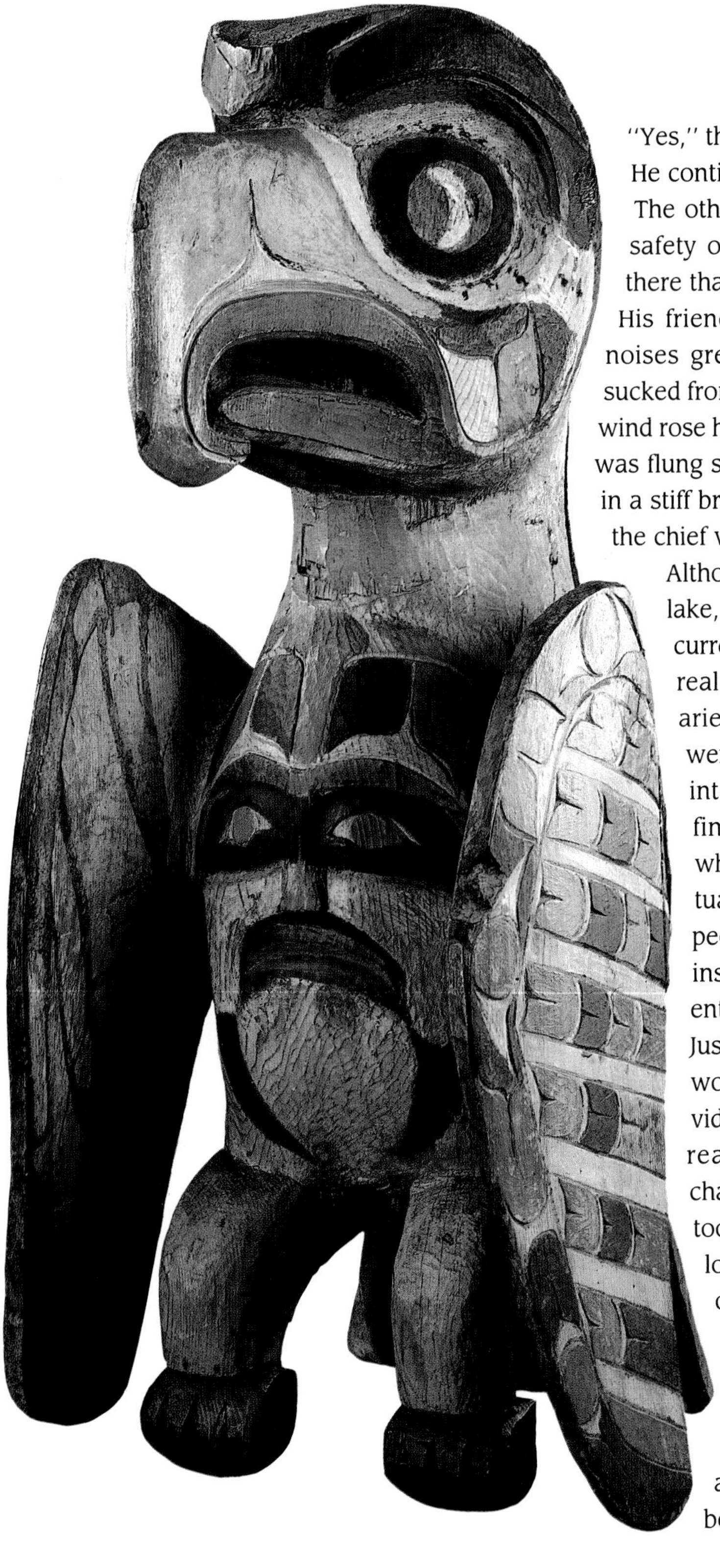

"Yes," the chief's son shouted back, "but it is nothing." He continued swimming.

The other boy pleaded with him to come back to the safety of land, crying out, "There is something bad there that we do not understand."

His friend ignored him, even though the mysterious noises grew louder. Then stones and branches were sucked from the shore and flew out into the water. As the wind rose higher, the boy on land grabbed a tree trunk. He was flung sideways, his legs fluttering like flags snapping in a stiff breeze. When the sucking died down, the son of the chief was nowhere to be found.

Although spirits inhabited specific sites, such as a lake, a mountain, or a place where violent ocean currents swirled, the geography of the supernatural realm was generally ill-defined, and the boundaries between the natural and the spirit world were often uncertain. People sometimes stumbled into a spirit village without warning, suddenly finding themselves surrounded by inhabitants who talked and looked like humans but were actually wolf or bear spirits. Many tales were told of people capsizing at sea or falling through ice and, instead of drowning, discovering that they had entered the land of the salmon or the seals.

Just as the geographic borders between the spirit world and the natural world were unclear, the dividing line between animal and human form was readily crossed. Not only did supernaturals change from animal to human shape, but people, too, could become animals if they lingered overly long among the supernaturals. The Kwakiutl tell of a woman who went to live in a lake because of difficulties with her husband. In time, she became a beaver and gave birth to beaver children. Her brothers begged her to return to her own world, and finally drained the lake in an effort to retrieve her. They found her on the bottom, covered with fur and no longer able to

speak, but still possessing a human face. Another Kwakiutl tale relates how killer whales abducted a woman and took her back to their village underneath the sea. Her husband managed to rescue her just as the whales were preparing to fit her with a dorsal fin that would have changed her into one of their own.

Despite the many legends describing the dangers of the supernaturals, spirit beings were as much helpmates as evildoers. Indeed, a number of rituals were designed to transform otherwise frightful or sinister creatures into benefactors. Monsters, predators, cannibals—all could become sources of strength for people who were bold enough to invoke such prodigious powers and put them to good use. The seeking of supernatural aid figured in countless activities, from hunting and fishing to fashioning a basket or canoe. Every trial and trouble, from the prospect of war to the onset of sickness, required a bid for favor. The bid could be a simple prayer, the use of a charm, or a visit to a sacred spot, such as a mountain where an ancient ancestor came down from the sky. To gain courage and invulnerability in battle, a war chief might bathe in salt water, said to be the home of supernatural sharks. Or he might seek help from a guardian spirit, identified in a vision, or through the medium of a shaman—a holy person with special links to the mysterious powers.

The protection of particular spirits could also come through inheritance. One of the great Northwest Coast ceremonies, the potlatch, held on important occasions such as the ascendancy of a new chief, reaffirmed the spirit-based wealth of a particular house. Some Northwest Coast peoples added another set of spiritual affiliations to the inheritance of the house—ties that were possessed by the initiates of secret societies and were celebrated by theatrical dances staged in the depths of winter, the most sacred season of the year.

Specific rituals and ceremonies varied from community to community. Among southern peoples, such as the Coast Salish and the Chinook, the most critical relations with spirits were personal, based on direct links forged between individuals and supernaturals. In the north, however, among the Tlingit, the Haida, and the Tsimshian, the principal ties to specific spirits were collective, ancestral legacies remembered in crests and masks and totem poles. In the central region, among the Nootka, the Bella Coola, and the Kwakiutl, both personal and household bonds existed, although the secret societies—distinct from families—provided one of the most important ways for power to flow into the human realm. Yet up and down the coast, from present-day Oregon to southern Alaska, the

The Nootka effigy at left also appears above with some 60 other figures at a Vancouver Island shrine whose purpose was to lure whales to the harpoon. The statues represent the bodies of whalers who were killed in battles with their quarry. Nootka chiefs ritually offered these symbolic remains as food to the spirits of dead whales in the hope of tempting the creatures to the hunter's boat. Nootka ancestors, acting through human skulls deposited at the shrine, used their powers to help entice the whales.

similarities in sacred practices far outweighed the differences. Whether it was expressed in private meditations or in great public dramas, a consciousness of supernatural forces was woven into every aspect of life among the peoples of the Northwest Coast. The spirits gave order to society, stitching together the past, the present, and the future.

Even the smallest activity required ritual cleanliness. When a craftsman prepared to make a canoe, he took great care to avoid any menstruating woman, including his wife, believing that such contact would weaken his tools and produce a flawed craft—or perhaps even injure the maker—because menstrual blood possessed a special power of its own and was taboo. Thus, at no time was a woman allowed to sit near a canoe that would be used in the hunting of seals, porpoises, and other sea mammals. Nor could such a canoe be used to convey dogs or a corpse.

Before setting out on an expedition, hunters fasted, bathed, and abstained from sexual intercourse in the belief that the game animals could sense any form of impurity—dirt on the skin, food in the belly, or the slightest trace of semen. A man never spoke of hunting prior to setting out because the animals also could comprehend human speech and might hear him. While the hunter was away, his wife helped him succeed in his endeavor by observing certain ritual precautions herself. For example, she might move as little as possible, speak in a quiet voice, avoid laughter, and keep apart from men.

Every hunter had his own rituals. Before going to sea, a Nootka whaler might rub his body with nettles, paint sacred marks on his face, and bathe in fresh water, swimming counterclockwise and mimicking the blowing sound of his prey. One renowned Nootka seal hunter prepared for an expedition by bathing in the ocean for four nights during the waxing moon. He began each night's ritual by rubbing himself with a particular seaweed. Next, he prayed in a loud voice, then slipped into the water and—to encourage his future quarry not to dive—swam with his head raised high for as long as he could bear the cold. He repeated the procedure 10 times each night.

Supernatural cooperation was essential for engaging in the most important of all Northwest Coast activities—salmon fishing. During most of the year, legends recounted, the salmon looked just like humans and lived in big houses beyond the horizon. But at a particular moment in the annual cycle, they assumed the trappings of fish and surged up the rivers and streams, offering their flesh but not their souls to the Indians. Their sacrifice was not automatic, however; humans had certain responsibilities. They needed to keep the river clean by not throwing rubbish into the water, and women of childbearing age were not allowed near the fishing areas because of possible menstrual contamination.

A similar sense of obligation underlay the rituals that most Indians of the region performed to honor the first salmon they caught each year. The Nootka, for example, brought the fish to the chief's house, placed them on newly woven mats with their heads pointing upriver, and sprinkled them with eagle down. The chief offered thanks on behalf of the peo-

Worn by a high-ranking Tlingit during the feast that followed the yearly salmon run, this highly stylized headdress features a human face and three bright red bars symbolizing salmon.

This intricately carved salmon rattle was used by the Tlingit in rituals that celebrated the annual salmon harvest. Various tribes held such rites to honor the fish and ensure its continued abundance.

ple. "We are glad you have come to visit us," he would say. "We have been saving these feathers for you for a long time. We hope you will return to visit us soon." The fish were then cooked and eaten in a general feast. Later, the bones of these fish—and, indeed, of all salmon subsequently taken—were returned to the water. This action enabled the salmon to return to the river the following year.

The Indians had similar rites reserved for game animals. Among the Coast Salish, the first elk to be killed each year was cut up and ceremoniously boiled, then shared by the entire village. In Nootka communities, a slain bear would be tied in an upright position behind a house. Offerings of freshly dried salmon would be laid on mats at its feet. Then a chief would sprinkle eagle down on the bear's head and say: "We have waited for you to visit us for a long time. Here is the eagle down you came to get." The Bella Coola ritual was slightly different. They would skin the bear, then place the pelt backward on the carcass, pat it four times, and say, "Tell your brothers, your sisters, your uncles, your aunts, and your other relations to come to me."

These carvings representing a canoe and two salmon played a part in the Tsimshian ritual held to welcome the salmon during the spawning season.

Even a tree had to be treated with respect. When the Tlingit cut timber to be used in the construction of a house, they lighted a fire close to the work site and threw food or oil into the flames to appease the tree spirits. Eagle down was scattered as a peace offering, helping to ensure that the felled trees did not injure their tree brethren as they came down. Sometimes the woodcutters would tell a tree that they had placed black bearskins on the ground to cushion its fall—although the skins were imaginary.

Every object and every phenomenon had a supernatural aspect susceptible to human appeal. If a raven cawed during a rainstorm, for example, the Indians might address it as a chief and ask the bird to intercede with the spirit responsible for bringing good weather. Special songs were sung to cause the wind to abate or increase; sea hunters recited prayers to bring storms, which were thought to drive the whales ashore. Even mountains were prayed to: A man walking beneath a cliff might beseech the mountain spirit and leave offerings to prevent a rock slide. Similarly, glaciers were believed to contain spirits capable of anger, and Indians always spoke softly when traveling near one.

Although relations between spirits and humans often concerned momentary needs or fluctuated according to the rhythms of life, the people of the Pacific Northwest also exhibited a keen sense of permanence in such matters. Ancestral connections between families and supernatural beings formed the enduring framework of their societies—a framework that was most carefully defined among the tribes living in the geographical area ranging from central British Columbia to southern Alaska. Those connections were cherished to the highest degree, and from time to time, a potlatch was staged to proclaim and explain them to an invited audience. Blending sacred and secular display of wealth, the potlatch was essentially a declaration of status—validated by the participation of the guests. Singing, dancing, feasting, and the distribution of goods were all part of the proceedings, and much of the celebration was festive. But other parts of the ceremony—a recapitulation of selfhood through song and dance, the wearing of crests, and the recitation of legends— were sacred. Fittingly, the very institution was rooted in the deep past.

A Bella Coola legend testifies to the potlatch's antiquity. At the beginning of time, the supreme deity took the form of the Sun (Sunx) and appeared to one of the first humans, who had made his home along the

Bella Coola River in a house of evergreen branches. While the man slept, the Sun built a salmon trap for him. After he awoke, the Sun appeared before him and conferred on him the name Sunxalotltha. "When you give a potlatch," the Sun said, "carve my face on your totem pole."

The Bella Coola mask shown here portrays at its center the life-giving sun. According to a legend handed down by the Bella Coola, the sun serves as a canoe for the supreme being, Althquntam, who journeys across the heavens while wearing a cloak lined with silvery salmon. The faces on the rim of the mask depict the Four Carpenters who constructed the world of the Bella Coola.

The Sun returned the next day and said, "I bring you the name Sunxakila. When you give a potlatch, carve my face on the bench where the chiefs sit."

The following day, the Sun appeared to the man once more and brought him a third name. "When you give a potlatch," the Sun instructed, "paint my face on the back wall of your house."

The day after that, the Sun arrived at the man's dwelling place again, this time in the guise of a stump with numerous roots that had been smoothed and polished by the flow of a river. On this occasion, he gave him a fourth name. That was the last visit.

In later years, when the earth had become populated, the man—now rich and revered—gave a series of potlatches. On each occasion, he used one of the names that the Sun had awarded him, and he displayed the Sun's image as instructed. In the last potlatch, he raised a bare stick as a totem pole, honoring the Sun's appearance as the water-polished stump of a tree.

Like so much else in the world of the Northwest Coast Indians, potlatches exhibited a rich variety. Some were relatively small affairs—little more than a neighborhood gathering, generally held in late summer or early fall, when food was abundant and travel easy. The reason for planning and executing such a potlatch could be almost any significant occasion in the cycle of life: the naming of a child, a girl's attainment of puberty, the time in a boy's life when he went to live with his maternal uncle, a marriage. In the Far North, Indians even gave potlatches as a way of erasing some small stain of shame. If, for example, a chief stumbled and fell during a ceremony, the damage to his honor could be undone by a giveaway of a few modest gifts at a public gathering—a minor form of potlatching.

Virtually all major potlatches were held for the same basic reason—to signify the inheritance of a chieftain's role. The head of a Coast Salish family might wait for several years before staging a potlatch to validate his accession. The Kwakiutl, Bella Coola, Nootka, and Haida, by contrast, gave potlatches well in advance of succession—at the time when a child was established as the heir presumptive. Among the Tlingit and some other northern peoples, the greatest potlatches were memorials, staged both to mourn the dead chief and to install his successor.

The mortuary rites of the Tlingit—the actual handling of the body of the deceased—were highly dramatic affairs. When an important personage died, the body remained in the house for a lengthy wake—four days in most cases, but eight days for a high-ranking chief. All Tlingit people belonged to one of two crest groups, either Ravens or Wolves, with children inheriting their mother's affiliation; the body of the deceased was prepared by members of the opposite group since the matrilineal kin of a chief were forbidden to touch the corpse. These helpers washed the body and painted the face with crest symbols. The deceased chief was then seated at the back of the house and bound in place. He wore mittens, moccasins, a wooden crest headdress, and a Chilkat blanket. His weapons and personal possessions were arrayed around him, and his slaves positioned close by. Over the next several days, the mourners—their hair cut, their faces painted black—would sing dirges and express their sorrow with speeches or keening. After the wake, the body was removed through a hole in the wall so that the living would not travel along the path of the dead as they went in and out of the door.

The Tlingit and the Tsimshian cremated the dead. The Haida, on the other hand, put the body of a chief in a grave house and later transferred the remains to a niche in the back of a mortuary pole or a box on the top of the pole. The Kwakiutl and the Nootka wrapped the dead in mats made of cedar bark and put them in boxes that were tied high in a tree or placed in a cave. The Coast Salish placed their noble dead in canoes lodged on platforms or in trees.

During the Tlingit cremation ceremony, members of the opposite crest group did the work. The body, covered with animal skins and blankets, was put on a pile of logs that had been packed with kindling and doused with seal or eulachon oil. Then the mourners—men facing the pyre and women sitting with their backs to it—sang clan-owned dirges as the flames consumed the body. (In the case of a prominent chief, a slave might be killed and cremated so that he or she might accompany the

At a mortuary potlatch about 1905, the body of an eminent Tlingit lies in state surrounded by possessions denoting his status. Draped over the body is a Chilkat blanket, a wool and cedar-bark weaving that was one of the most prestigious items a man could own. Hats depicting various family crests proclaim the noble lineage of the deceased.

chief to the next world.) Afterward, the ashes and bones of the deceased were put in a box for temporary storage.

A year or so later, the remains were shifted to another box and placed in a grave house or mortuary pole—an event known as Finishing the Body. A memorial potlatch followed. This ceremony signified the final dissolution of the deceased, but the concept of dissolution, like so much else in the life of the Northwest Coast peoples, was subtle and complex. The Tlingit believed that a dead person was not one entity but several, each with a different destination. The ghost of the deceased was thought to settle where the remains were stored. Another spirit component went to a permanent home in the village of the dead—a place located some-

In 1894 at Fort Rupert on Vancouver Island, guests at a Kwakiutl potlatch look on as an elegantly attired chief lavishes praise upon their host. Elaborate speeches thanking the host for his generosity were a traditional and prescribed part of potlatch ceremonies.

where far away. Still another component was reincarnated as a baby born to a close matrilineal female relative before the memorial potlatch. Finally, there was the issue of the dead person's possessions. In the case of a deceased chief, his names and crests, his senior wife, and his title and wealth all went to his successor at the memorial potlatch.

The lineage of the deceased sponsored the memorial potlatch, usually with the aid of other local lineages of the clan. One of the ceremony's purposes was symbolically to connect the living members of the lineage with the dead. To that end, the most important physical expression of the lineage—the house—was restored or rebuilt, a job performed by members of the opposite crest group. Their work on the house, along with the services provided at the time of death, placed the dead chief's lineage in their debt. Repayment came in the form of the gifts distributed at the potlatch. The gifts were also viewed as payment to the guests for listening to the lamentations of the hosts and for acting as witnesses to the ritual declarations of the lineage's rights to their crests, songs, dances, and names. The attendance of the guests, who invariably included both neighbors and high-ranking in-laws from other villages, validated the status and vitality of the change in leadership.

The Tlingit always held important potlatches in late fall or early winter, when larders were full. The event took many days—typically, four days of secular entertainment, one or two of ritual, and then several more of feasting and dancing. But a lengthy preparation time was planned so that the sponsors could accumulate the wealth that would be given to the guests and rehearse their songs and dances. Because the guests, too, had to prepare songs and dances, invitations were usually issued many months in advance, often as much as a year. The brothers-in-law of the deceased notified the guests. Shortly before the potlatch, these same men went forth again to escort the out-of-town guests to the village where the ceremony would be held.

The approach of the guests followed a precisely defined course. They camped for one night at a site near the village that had been prepared by the hosts; in the meantime, the brothers-in-law hurried ahead to announce the guests' impending arrival. When the outsiders reached the village the next day, they danced on the beach as guests from the local area looked on from war canoes. Then the two groups exchanged places, with the locals taking a turn at dancing while the out-of-towners watched them from the canoes. At that point, the host chief formally welcomed everyone into the house where the potlatch would take place.

The following four days were devoted to costumed entertainments and various forms of lighthearted competition among the guests—singing and dancing contests, or trials of who could eat the most food or drink the most seal oil. Next came the potlatch proper. To start this phase, the host chief gave a speech explaining the reasons for the potlatch. Then, for hours, he and the other hosts, all dressed in ancestral regalia, lamented the loss of their relative. They sang ancient mourning songs, wailed and wept, and made special sounds that signified the expelling of sadness from their bodies. Periodically, high-ranking guests stood up and delivered speeches of comfort, and at intervals, both hosts and guests relieved the atmosphere of sorrow by dancing.

Then the mood changed. The guests ate food that symbolically contained the spiritual essence of the hosts' ancestors; some of the food was placed in the fire by the hosts as the family names were pronounced. The hosts then put on special potlatch hats and other regalia that displayed their crests. (The Tsimshian and Kwakiutl sometimes wore masks as well.) This was a critical moment: For the first time, the host chief donned the ceremonial regalia of his deceased predecessor, thus officially assuming his position. He and other clan members also took on new names.

In a series of stories, songs, and dances, the hosts described their family history for the guest witnesses: how they had acquired privileges and power from supernatural beings, and how they had come to possess the wealth visible in the house—the beautiful serving dishes fashioned in the shape of crest animals, the elaborately carved spoons and bentwood boxes, the endless stores of food. The stories themselves and the other modes of performance were also possessions. Only the keepers of a crest were allowed to recount how the crest was obtained. The Tlingit owner of the Golden Eagle crest, for example, might say words like these—recorded in modern times:

Now you are going to hear from us about our origin and destiny. We are Teqwedi. You will hear the song about the place where we have our land. This happened way up at the head of Ahrnklin River. One of our ancestors was out hunting in the mountains at the head of Ahrnklin, and he came upon that Golden Eagle. As he was coming toward it, he heard it singing. That was why he walked toward the place from where the song was coming. As soon as the bird saw the man, it began to sing in Tlingit, and he could understand it. The man saw that Golden Eagle

THE POTENT MAGIC
OF THE MASK

For the people of the Northwest Coast, the world teems with spirits that dwell within every facet of nature: great whales, spawning fish, and the chill waters that carry them; raven, wind, sun, and all the powers and residents of the sky; the mist-shrouded forests, and the sundry creatures that stalk their quarry or seek shelter from pursuit in the deep shadows.

A vital force pervades every fiber of existence, from stones that can only tumble down the flanks of mountains to the echoes that fill the valleys when they fall. And for every spirit, there is a corresponding face, reflecting the interwoven genealogies of man, animal, earth, and their supernatural forebears. The world of these Northwest Coast tribes abounds in faces, whether worked into household articles or gazing out from towering poles, but none of these stylized visages holds the power that resides in masks.

Masterpieces of the carver's skill and inspiration, masks enable dancers and shamans to personify the deities, creatures, and forces evoked during the sacred ceremonies and curing rituals. No two masks are the same, yet each bears features that for generations have faithfully invoked the presence of a spiritual guest. The potent magic of the faces on these masks opens a portal to the invisible world, where fabulous beings play out immortal dramas.

An aura of gentle serenity emanates from this Tsimshian lunar mask, whose carver might have been inspired by a similar face that he saw in the moon.

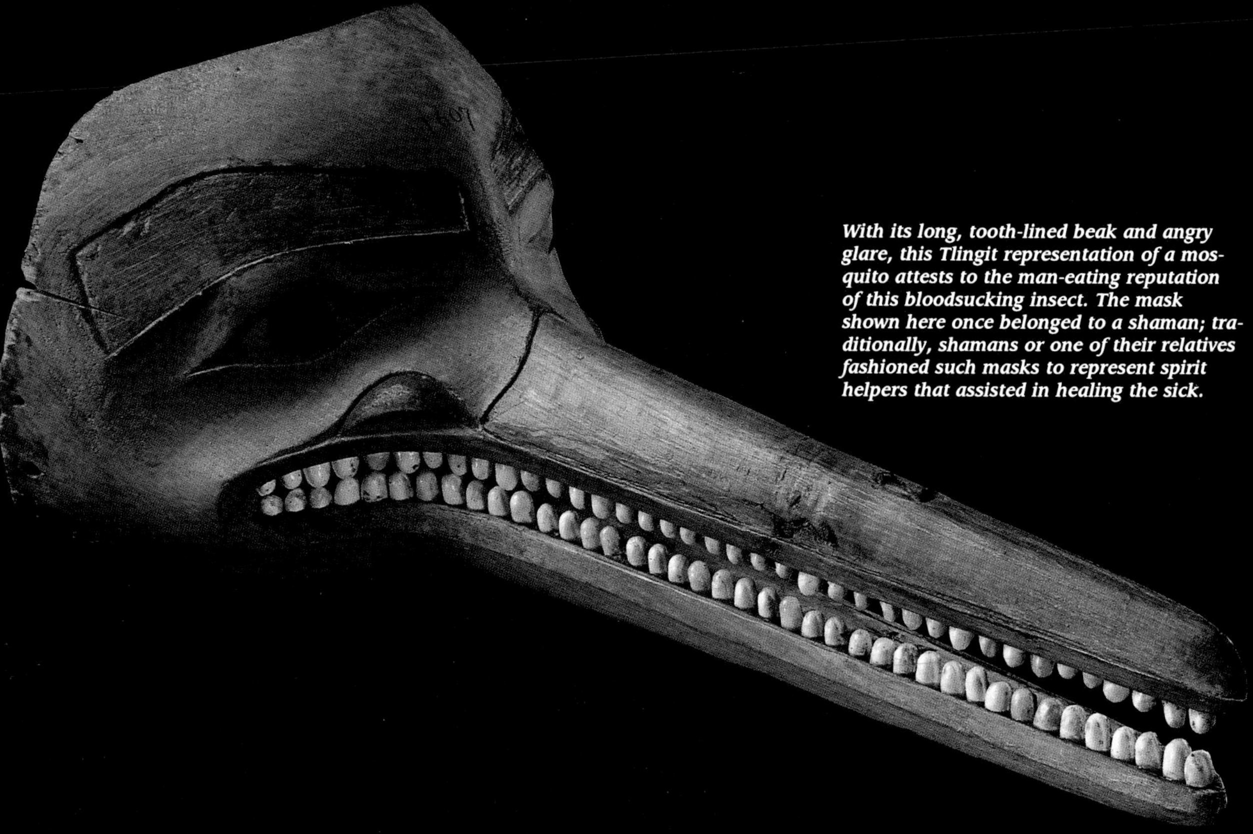

With its long, tooth-lined beak and angry glare, this Tlingit representation of a mosquito attests to the man-eating reputation of this bloodsucking insect. The mask shown here once belonged to a shaman; traditionally, shamans or one of their relatives fashioned such masks to represent spirit helpers that assisted in healing the sick.

Sisiutl, a supernatural being associated with warriors, is depicted as two serpent heads joined by a horned, humanlike face. Capable of turning enemies to stone with his gaze and invulnerable to weapons, he is fearsome in battle, but like many ferocious spirits, he also bestows status and riches. This Kwakiutl mask features movable snakes' heads and retractable tongues to enhance the drama of its appearance.

This Haida mask has stylized black feathers fanning out from its chin that symbolize the spirit Raven, the great trickster and teacher. Indians of the Pacific Northwest have always believed that animal spirits were capable of transforming themselves into humans.

This mask depicts a
lake-dwelling pro-
tector spirit of the
Coast Salish whose
birdlike face with
protruding ears is
crowned by animal
heads and a stand
of feathers. Owner-
ship of such masks
has been restricted
to select families
who bring them out
to sanctify impor-
tant social events.

As part of the
Nootka Shamans
Dance, initiates
wear this mask with
a wolf head sur-
mounting a human
face during their rit-
ual abduction by
wolf spirits, patrons
of Nootka lore and
ceremony. While
captives, the novices
are instructed in he-
reditary lore, which
they then bring
back to their people.

was holding two baby groundhogs. It had broken its wing trying to catch those little groundhogs. The bird did not want to be killed, so in place of its life, it gave that song to the man. He listened until he learned it by heart. That is how the old people came to know it. They never like to kill anything in a wounded condition. And that is why the bird gave the man that song in place of its life.

Then the man came to the bird, set the wing, and put it in a dry cave. That bird was intended to be the origin and destiny of the Ahrnklin Teqwedi.

How many hundreds of years the people were living before us? But the history of what happened to them has been handed down from generation to generation. That is why we know it.

This is the song I want to sing, so everybody can hear it. If anyone belonging to the Drum House People hears this song, anywhere in the world, he will know who he is, and from whom he is descended. That is all. I am going to sing: "I come from the other side of the mountain. / From where the sun rises, it is beginning to be light. / The dawn of morning is coming from the other side of the mountain."

To ensure the good health and fortune of their clients, Tlingit shamans often gave them charms like the one above, which depicts in ivory a shaman and one source of his spiritual power, an octopus. The Tlingit believed shamans had a vast array of even more potent spirit helpers whose powers could not be tapped by laymen alone.

At the climax of the potlatch, the gifts were brought into the house. All of the hosts, including the children, made some donation to the guests. As they did so, they sang a clan song or spoke again of their sorrow for the deceased, and again the guests offered comfort with songs, dances, and speeches. The gifts took many forms. Some might be as simple as cedar bark for weaving, but furs, blankets, canoes, and even slaves were also given away. The most precious gifts of all were pieces of metal known as coppers. These flat, shield-shaped objects were originally made from native ore, but by the middle of the 19th century, most of them were fashioned from copper obtained from whites through the fur trade. Coppers were owned by chiefs, but possession was vested in the entire household. The front of a copper was adorned with a crest, usually created by a two-step imaging process: First, the surface was blackened by smoking it over a resinous fire or covering it with a mixture of grease, spruce gum, and powdered charcoal; the crest design was then scratched on this darkened field to reveal the gleaming metal underneath.

Potlatch gifts were always distributed on the basis of the recipient's rank: Chiefs received more than commoners. The gifting process thus was a detailed assertion of the social order, expressing not just the position of the house and its new chief but also fine degrees of prestige among those who had been invited. The brothers-in-law who had been responsible for extending the invitations and escorting the guests handled the distribution. They called each recipient by name and described the nature and value of the gift. Later, the guests thanked their hosts in speeches. These final feasts might last four days. Then, the guests set out for home, laden with their bounty and a lavish farewell offering of food. Back in their homes, chiefs shared the gifts they had been given with other members of their household.

Among groups living in the southern region of the Northwest Coast, affiliations with supernatural beings tended to be an individual matter. Everyone—men and women, nobles, commoners, and even slaves—attempted to acquire one or more guardian spirits who would remain with them for life. Guardian spirits came in a limitless variety of animals, fish, birds, insects, and amphibians. They could also be seemingly inanimate beings or forces of nature. All of the guardian spirits provided specific benefits. The wolf spirit, for example, made a man a skilled hunter of deer, elk, and bear. A woman whose guardian spirit was a female spider would be an expert weaver. The mink spirit conferred the power to catch fish. The fly spirit helped a hunter find game. The west wind spirit made a man a great warrior and enabled him to summon good weather.

Theoretically, any individual could acquire almost any kind of guardian spirit, although a few of the supernatural helpers were associated only with specific occupations. In practice, family tradition narrowed the choice: Most people obtained spirits that had belonged to their ancestors. The manner of acquisition could take several forms. In certain cases, it was inadvertent. People spoke of being repeatedly "jumped" by spirits, thereby gaining an array of special abilities. A person mourning a dead relative or walking in a lonely place might gain a guardian spirit without even knowing it—although a shaman could later reveal the spirit's identity. But in most cases, a spirit was actively sought, through either a special ceremony or a spiritual journey known as a vision quest.

The Coast Salish Guardian Spirit Ceremony consisted of a multiday rite in which older dancers mediated the transfer of ancestral spirit power to a young man or woman. Often the ceremony was arranged by the

A DISTINCTIVE ARTISTRY

Northwest Coast Indians have habitually decorated everything they possess, from their humblest housewares to their most sacred regalia, with stylized images of creatures both mythical and real. The simplest renderings tend to be realistic, and the animal being depicted is easily recognizable.

In more abstract compositions, the artist has rearranged some features, discarded others, and distorted still others, thus making his subject unidentifiable to the untutored eye. Fortunately, most artists have included conventional animal symbols to aid the viewer. For example, the prominent incisors and crosshatched tail of the animal on the 19th-century Tsimshian dance apron at left are standard symbols of the beaver.

In spite of such visual cues, the meaning of some compositions is obscure to outsiders. The beauty of such art is nonetheless accessible to all.

youth's father, and the dancers were hired for the occasion. The transfer was achieved in stages. One night, the dancers would carry the youth around the house, chanting "Hu! hu! hu!" and breathing on the initiate; then each dancer sang his own song and performed his own dance to the rhythms of drums and sticks. These dances were repeated in front of the community each morning and evening for the next three days. At some point, the youth would feel the presence of a spirit and begin to chant. Everyone listened carefully until an elder identified the spirit by the sounds issuing from the initiate. Then the whole house would erupt with chanting and drumming as people joined in the youngster's song. Later, those who claimed to have the same kind of guardian spirit would teach the initiate the proper steps of the spirit dance. On the last day of the ceremony, the youth was roused to a frenzy by drumbeats and had to be restrained by attendants, who painted the initiate's face with red ocher or black grease. Then they set off together into the woods, where the attendants enacted certain rites before leading the youth back to the village. There the proud youngster performed the spirit dance and ate a ceremonial meal to celebrate the transfer of power. The ceremony concluded with feasting and gift giving.

A more typical path to spirit acquisition was the vision quest—the personal pursuit of direct supernatural contact during the course of solitary vigils. Such a vision usually came before the onset of puberty. Children were trained for the rigors of the quest from a young age. To learn cleanliness and self-discipline, they began bathing daily, even in cold weather, when they were only five or six years old. Throughout childhood, they were taught which spirits favored their family line. Grandparents and other adults created exercises to help them overcome their fear of the spirit-filled woods: The child might be asked to go out at night to retrieve some small object that had been placed on a hilltop, beside a lake, or where the waves beat against a rocky point.

Usually about the age of 10, boys and girls began questing. Ritually purified and touching no food, they would stay out in the woods for days at a time. On one of these vigils, a spirit would contact the child, perhaps after first announcing its presence with a sound.

Most seekers received instructions telling them how to deal with this potentially terrifying experience. As one Lower Chinook woman recalled the advice given to her: "You may hear a voice, but don't run away. Stay and listen. Then when you start home, don't run, just walk slowly. If you pass a pool or a stream, stop and swim. Dive five times. Then if you are tired, lie down, but be sure you are on the side of the water toward home. If you hear a voice again, don't be frightened. Stay and listen. The spirit will not cross the water; it will stay on the other side. It will be an animal when you first see it, but it will change and look like a man. It will tell you what power you will have and what you are to do when you are grown."

After a successful vision quest, the child said almost nothing about the encounter. Indeed, a kind of mystical forgetfulness ensued; the experience was washed from memory and remained beyond the reach of the conscious mind for years. Nor was the guardian spirit active during this period: Men and women were not directly aided by their supernatural ally

Having donned his ceremonial regalia and sprinkled himself with sacred eagle down, this Tlingit shaman is ready to perform a healing ritual (below). In each hand he grasps a rattle he will use to summon his spirit helpers, who on arriving will greatly amplify the shaman's curative powers.

until they reached maturity—considered to be the early thirties for women and the late thirties for men—the age when parents traditionally became grandparents. Even then, they were aware of their guardian spirit only during the winter—the time of year when it was believed that supernatural beings drew close to humans. Feelings of uneasiness or of sick-

ness were a signal of the nearness of a supernatural power, and the feelings could be relieved only by performing a dance and singing a song that the guardian spirit had revealed to the seeker years earlier. All along the southern part of the Northwest Coast, the greatest ceremonies held during the winter months were dances executed in honor of guardian spirits.

Rings woven of cedar bark and a headdress inlaid with abalone shell are among the items that make up this shaman's kit. Some of the objects—the necklaces of long ivory pendants (left foreground), for example, and the raven rattle propped against the wooden storage chest—are similar to those used and worn by the shaman (inset). When a shaman died, his kit was interred with him to prevent its powers from being unleashed.

This Nootka shaman's rattle consists of dozens of tiny wooden fish suspended within a framework of wooden dowels. Some two feet square, the rattle was used in dances that were performed before fishing trips to stimulate the generosity of the fish spirits.

To some persons—in most cases male—the spirits gave power far beyond the usual measure. Such individuals became shamans and were regarded with awe and fear by others. Shamans generally achieved their close ties to the supernatural by means of an intensified version of the vision quest. The fasting was longer, the physical mortification more severe, and the commitment to ritual purity more rigorous. Nor could a shaman ever depart from a strict regimen of purification and penance; otherwise, the spirits would regard his body as an unsuitable receptacle of their power.

The shaman functioned as an intermediary between humans and the supernatural realm, peering into the spirit world and sometimes ritually traveling there. Because of his ability to penetrate the boundaries of the supernatural, he could perform extraordinary feats—cure illness, ensure success in war, control the weather, and see across time or space to bring news of the future or of events happening far away.

Ready access to the supernatural was a frightening gift. So great was the power hovering about a shaman that it could be dangerous for a person with a weak guardian spirit to come close to him. The lesser person's power might be attracted to the shaman and stick to him; worse, the very soul of the person might be drawn away, resulting in a life-threatening

illness. Touching a shaman's ritual paraphernalia—his rattle, wand, or bone necklace—was also exceedingly risky, and remained so even after the shaman's death. Among the Tlingit and other northern coastal groups who cremated their dead, a deceased shaman was exempted from the funeral pyre; instead, his body was laid on a board in a grave house, as though sleeping. It was said that the body did not decay but simply dried up, retaining its supernatural power. No prudent person would go near a shaman's grave house. Merely drinking from a nearby stream or picking berries in the vicinity was considered to be perilous.

Near an Alaskan village, wooden guardians watch over the nearby grave of a Tlingit shaman. The Tlingit believed that a shaman's remains held powers that could be wielded for evil by witches and malevolent spirits, and they erected wooden sentinels to drive off interlopers. The figure at right, which also appears on the left above, wears the garb of a shaman; the rattles that he once carried have long since disappeared, but he still chants a protective prayer.

Shamanism usually ran in families. It was sometimes said to pass from one generation to another by contagion. Often the telltale signs appeared at an early age (although the calling could come at any time). In a family with an inherited tendency to shamanism, parents watched their children for moods or events that suggested a latent talent for it. If a boy was dreamy and kept apart from his fellows, for example, he might become a shaman. Falling into a fit was considered an indication of susceptibility to supernatural power. The most specific augury, however, was a visitation by a mouse, a creature the Indians depicted as speaking all languages and having access to all peoples; if a young person heard a voice calling during sleep and awoke to see a mouse disappearing, he would probably grow up to be a shaman.

The road to shamanhood was arduous, involving years of penance and extensive training. A particularly detailed account of the apprenticeship was provided by a Coast Salish shaman who grew up along the lower Fraser River in the mid-19th century: "When I was only three years old, my mother, who was herself a medicine woman, made me bathe in the river and scrub my limbs with spruce boughs before breakfast, even though there was ice on the water. One morning after I had scrubbed myself, she clothed me with her power. Every living creature possesses its special power, something invisible to normal eyes that dwells inside it, and yet can issue from it, giving it power to do the thing it wishes to do. Well, that morning she clothed me with her power; she passed her hands over my body, from head to feet, draping her strength over me to shield and fortify me for the trials that she projected for me later."

Until this shaman-to-be was 10 years of age, his boyhood followed the usual course; he played like other children and learned the skills of hunting and fishing from adults. But his destiny would be different. One morning, his mother roused him from bed and said: "It is time now that you trained to become a medicine man. Go back into the woods, but be careful that no one sees you. Whenever you come to a pool, bathe, and rub yourself with spruce boughs, then walk on again. Stay out as long as you can. Remember that He Who Dwells Above has given you power. Pray to Him as you walk along; ask His help; plead with Him to strengthen you for the trials you must now undergo."

The boy did as he was told, and on subsequent days his mother sent him back into the forest, without food. At first he stayed there only until dark, but soon he was sleeping in the woods. Other shamans started to teach him their arts, and they urged him to lengthen his vigils. He spent much of the next four winters alone, fasting and purifying himself. Then one day, a vision came to him:

"I had been dancing and had fallen to the ground exhausted. As I lay there, sleeping, I heard a medicine man singing far, far away, and my mind traveled toward the voice. Evil medicine men seemed to swarm around me, but always there was someone behind me who whispered, 'Pay no attention to them, for they are evil.' And I prayed constantly to Him Who Dwells Above, asking for power to heal the sick, not to cause sickness as did these evil ones.

"I reached the place where the medicine man was singing, a house unlike any that I had ever seen before. He who was behind me whispered, 'Go inside. This is he for whom you are seeking, the true medicine man for whom you have undergone penance all these years.'

"I entered. The medicine man was kneeling on the floor, and beside him was his water in some mystic vessel that was neither a dish nor a basket. He turned and looked at me. 'Poor boy,' he said. 'So you have come at last. Kneel down beside me.'

"I knelt beside him. In front of us appeared every sickness that afflicts mankind, concentrated in a single human being. 'Wash your hands and wrists in this water.' I washed them. He grasped them in his own and massaged them, giving them power. 'Now lay your hands on that sickness and remove it.' I laid my hands to the patient and cupped his sickness out with them. He rose to his feet, cured. 'That is how you shall remove every sickness. You shall chant the song you have heard me sing and cup out the sickness with your hands. Now go.' "

Some shamans came much later to their calling—and in a few cases with no particular preparation. One Nootka woman—a member of a family with many shamans—did not have her first supernatural encounter until she was an adult. One day when she was carrying a bucket to a spring, she heard an odd noise and saw a log that appeared to be moving, with a squirrel scurrying back and forth along its length like a shaman busily attending to a sick person. The log gave a groan, causing her to faint. The squirrel was still there when she awoke, but she drove it away and stilled the log by uttering a ritual cry. That night and for many to come, she heard songs in her dreams.

Awhile later, she went to a beach to gather driftwood. Suddenly she saw two wolves sitting close by, and again she fainted. When she regained consciousness, the wolves were gone. Inspecting the spot where the animals had lurked, she found no tracks, but she came across a peb-

The wooden heads attached to this cedar-bark apron indicate that its owner was a member of the Hamatsa, or Cannibal, Society. During their annual winter ceremony, this group reenacted the ancient encounter between ancestors of the Kwakiutl and the Cannibal at the North End of the World.

ble covered with fresh blood. Her mother instructed her to go into the woods to bathe and rub herself with herbs and sing. Later, her grandfather—a shaman—sang over her in order to "fix her power."

Following their initial vision, most shamans went through a period of training, practicing the songs and dances that they learned in dreams; this period of apprenticeship might last from a few months to many years. Afterward, they were ready to devote themselves to their principal work and the source of their prestige—curing sicknesses. Illness was thought to have several possible causes. The most common was the presence of tiny, semianimate objects in the patient's body, shot there by witches, perhaps, or by angry spirits. The shaman first located the object and then ritually drew it to the surface through protracted chanting and sucking, as helpers drummed in the background; at the moment when the chanting and drumming reached a crescendo, the evil agent was extracted.

Diseases could also be caused by ghosts visiting from the land of the dead. A wandering ghost might become hungry for food from its living relatives; when a relative failed to respond, the ghost might retaliate by introducing a sickness. Fortunately, a shaman could often make contact with the ghost and satisfy it by placing food for the spirit in a fire.

Yet another reason for sickness was the loss of the soul. Sometimes a person's soul was stolen by a ghost; sometimes it simply strayed away. To retrieve the invisible but critical component of being, a shaman would travel into the spirit world, an expedition dramatized by singing and dancing. The ceremonial journey lasted all night. Among most groups, shamans made these mystical trips alone, but shamans around Puget Sound sometimes worked in teams for the most critical cases. Villagers would gather in a large communal house for a ritual called the Soul Recovery Ceremony, aimed at curing an individual who was wasting away. It was the most complex of all Coast Salish rites, with much feasting, gift giving, speechmaking, chanting, and drumming. The core of the ceremony was a pantomimed canoe voyage to the land of the dead. The Indians held the ceremony in the months of December and January because they perceived the land of the dead as the reverse of the natural world. Thus, cold winter darkness indicated a beautiful summer day in the afterworld.

To make the voyage, an even number of shamans was needed. They formed a single row in the center of the house, representing the crew of a canoe. Behind each shaman was a cedar board bearing an image of his guardian spirit. All of the shamans held long poles that served variously as paddles, weapons, walking sticks, or drumsticks. The shaman in the

Wearing carved wooden masks, Hamatsa Dancers portray Raven (left) and Hokhokw (right), two of the three supernatural birds who helped Cannibal at the North End of the World. Raven, it was said, plucked out and devoured the eyes of humans while Hokhokw cracked open their skulls with its powerful beak and ate the brains inside.

bow of the imaginary canoe initiated the voyage with a song; the man in the stern steered; and the others, aided by the spectators, hastened the journey by singing songs.

As the shamans sang, they made an excursion in their minds, following the route that souls travel after death. Two rivers marked the journey. The first one was so turbulent and filled with obstacles that the shamans—like the souls that had preceded them—had to cross by means of a fallen log. The second river could be traversed by canoe, and on the far bank was the village of the dead. There, men and women lived as they had on earth, but many things in this realm were reversed—day and night, the sequence of the seasons, the ebb and flow of the tides.

In order to learn the location of the soul they sought to bring back with them, the shamans questioned a ghost whom they captured while it

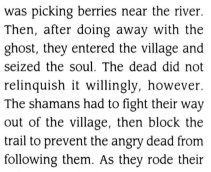

was picking berries near the river. Then, after doing away with the ghost, they entered the village and seized the soul. The dead did not relinquish it willingly, however. The shamans had to fight their way out of the village, then block the trail to prevent the angry dead from following them. As they rode their spirit canoe back to the world of the living, they broke into song. If they had retrieved the correct soul, the patient would rise up and slowly begin to dance and sing. If not, the shamans might attempt another journey.

In the four early-20th-century photographs shown on this page and opposite, young Kwakiutl men undergo initiation rites for membership in the Hamatsa Society. In the two photographs above, one of the initiates performs a dance while wearing hemlock boughs on his head and around his waist and wrists as signs of his untamed state.

In the central region of the Northwest Coast, the most important winter ceremonies were staged by secret societies. These organizations represented a sort of alternate social structure, replacing the clan during the months of darkness and rain; people dropped their summer names and assumed winter names, and their identity was now bound up with the prerogatives of their religious societies—made up of groups of initiates who each derived power from a particular patron spirit and honored that spirit with a special dance. The performers and their distinctive dances formed a hierarchy. In one Kwakiutl dancing society, for example, the highest rank was that of Cannibal Dancer, known as Hamatsa; below were Fire Throwing Dancer, Grizzly Bear Dancer, Rat Spirit Dancer, Chewing Spirit Dancer, and on down a list that included dozens of dancers in all, among them such minor spirits as Door Guarding Spirit and Spirit Playing at the Tide Line. This sacred season ranking paralleled the social hierarchy of the secular season, since the most prominent people performed the most important dances.

The winter ceremonies were initiations, held in a house especially prepared for the purpose and typically sponsored—at considerable expense—by the father or grandfather of the initiate. The dramatic effects were masterful, involving the use of masks with movable parts, tunnels or trapdoors that allowed a performer to materialize out of nowhere, twine-strung wooden figures that seemed to fly across the house, and hollow strands of kelp that served as speaking tubes. For a winter ceremony rite called the Ghost Dance, hollow kelp tubes were laid under the floor and terminated in the fire; the Ghost Dancer circled the fire, then vanished into a ditch and began a journey to the lower world, escorted by

Possessed by the spirit of Cannibal at the North End of the World, a novice cries out for human flesh (left). As the spirit departs and he is gradually transformed into a human again, his handlers drape rings woven of cedar bark around his neck and over a shoulder (right) to restrain him. Only relatively high-ranking members of the Hamatsa Society were allowed to wear cedar-bark head rings such as the one below.

ghosts whose voices were heard speaking from the flames. In another dance that mimicked a spirit shooting disease into people, the dancer handled a "worm"—a stick that seemed to change its size; at one point, the worm appeared to fly through the air under its own power, an illusion created as two men, hidden on either side of the house, pulled a stick across the room by means of a long string. Later, the dancer rid himself of the worm by appearing to vomit it out, along with a copious flow of blood that actually emanated from a bladder held inside his mouth.

All the dance series followed the same basic plot: A novice encounters a spirit and is kidnapped; the spirit subsequently endows the novice with supernatural power and sends him back to his village. These events were seen as a re-creation of an ancestral encounter; in effect, the dancer was establishing himself as the heir to the dance, the possessor of the spirit's mystical force.

The playing out of the plot was frequently wild and terrifying, and never was this more true than in the performance of the Cannibal Dance, whose empowering spirit was a supernatural by the name of Baxbaxwalanuxsiwe—Cannibal at the North End of the World. The origins of this particular dance lay buried deep in the past, but each performance of it rendered the mythical events frighteningly immediate. No matter how many times onlookers may have witnessed the dance, the drama unfolds before them as if for the first time.

During a feast day in a Kwakiutl village at Fort Rupert on Vancouver Island in 1894, men of the Hamatsa Society sit proudly on an elevated platform, a position of honor. The group's high-ranking members have blackened their faces with charcoal, donned cedar-bark head and neck rings, and sprinkled eagle down on their heads to indicate their status. Other prominent villagers take seats below the society's vanguard.

A month or so before the dance is due to take place, the novice—usually a male—becomes inspired and runs along the beach crying, "Hap! hap! hap!" Attendants chase after him, but he disappears—metaphorically kidnapped (although in truth, the novice retreats to a house, cave, or woodland shelter where he receives instruction in the ways of the society). When all is in readiness for the ceremony, his terrifying Cannibal cry is heard near the village, and the attendants hurry out to capture him. By this time, he is in a kind of frenzy, filled with the power of Cannibal at the North End of the World. In the dance house, he faints at the sight of some Cannibal masks that have not been properly made. Attendants revive him by blowing water over his body, chanting, shaking their rattles, and performing other procedures, including the destruction of the faulty masks in the fire. Since he is still in a maddened state, they tie him to a pole to restrain him.

That night, he gets free and disappears again. He is recaptured the next morning, and all the events of the previous day are repeated. The following day and night, he dances for the other society members. On the fourth day, after a potlatch, the dancer suddenly appears in the room and begins biting people, fighting off the efforts of attendants to stop him. His hunger for human flesh appears to be overwhelming, and the attendants finally decide to appease him by bringing in a corpse—traditionally, either the body of a deceased relative, carefully prepared by drying it, or a convincing substitute such as a skinned bear or a mannequin. (Human flesh is not actually consumed.)

The ritual consumption of the corpse has the desired effect, and subsequently the Cannibal Dancer is taken to the shore and washed. He is then brought back to the house and dressed in a bearskin robe and apron; large rings of dyed cedar bark are placed on his head, neck, wrists, and ankles. He becomes more subdued in his movements as four female attendants tame the spirit in him with supernatural songs.

The final phase of the ceremony is the naming of the Cannibal Dancer. Several false names are whispered to him until he hears one that is taboo and cries, "Hap! hap! hap!" before fainting away. When he wakes, the female attendants must again drive the agitated spirit out of him. At last, he is ready to receive his rightful name, passed down like all titles from generation to generation. In this manner, the initiate and everyone present are reminded once more of the central facts of Northwest Coast sacred belief—that past and present are indissolubly tied, and that fearful and wondrous powers lie just a few steps away, waiting. ❖

THE VILLAGES WITHOUT HOPE

Among the status-conscious societies of the Pacific Northwest, few were as conspicuously well-to-do as the Haida of the Queen Charlotte Islands. These bold seafaring traders called their 150-island archipelago off the coast of British Columbia Haida Gwaii, literally, Islands of the People. Along its convoluted shorelines, they proudly displayed their wealth by building the most imposing dwellings and erecting the tallest, most numerous totem poles on the coast.

But the proud, self-reliant Haida were cruelly vulnerable to European-borne disease. In 1774, when the first foreigners arrived at Haida Gwaii, there were perhaps 34 villages there. Hemmed in by dense forests, most of the communities could be reached only by sea, a condition that isolated their residents and fostered a fierce sense of loyalty to clan and place. In less than a century, influenza, measles, whooping cough, scarlet fever, tuberculosis, venereal disease—and especially smallpox—had devastated those self-contained communities, reducing a population of 7,000 to fewer than 1,000. Said one despairing chief after a smallpox epidemic in 1862, "Now the fires have gone out, and the brave men have fallen before the iron man's sickness."

Gradually, those who remained packed their belongings and left their home villages. Once-flourishing towns such as Ninstints and Skedans, whose weather-bleached ruins are shown here, grew quiet and empty. By the end of the 19th century, all the survivors had gathered in Skidegate and Massett, two towns served by Christian missionaries. Yet the flinty islanders still nourished their strong ties to clan and property. Year after year, the Haida continued to return to their old uninhabited villages, using them as camps for hunting and fishing. Even today, descendants of Haida lineages sing the songs, tell the stories, and recount the names associated with each site, still claiming the vanished ancestral homes of Haida Gwaii as part of their living heritage.

Dixon Entrance

Yan
Massett

BRITISH COLUMBIA

Hecate Strait

Skidegate

Skedans

PACIFIC OCEAN

Ninstints

Scale of Miles
0   25   50   75   100

Tom Price and John Robson, descendants of
two Haida noble houses, wear the ceremonial attire of
their inherited rank. Price was the last chief to live
in Ninstints before the villagers left in 1875.

Women and children stand in front of a raven crest in Yan, a small village on the west shore of Massett Inlet. A few years after this picture was taken in 1881, the community was ravaged by smallpox; within a decade, the survivors had all moved to the town of Massett.

*Master of a vanishing craft, Massett boatbuilder Alfred Davidson
works on the bow of a cedar canoe in 1914. Large, seagoing Haida canoes were
important trade items, valued throughout the northern Pacific Coast
until replaced by European-style fishing boats.*

Haida fishermen harvest herring eggs as their ancestors did, lifting roe-laden hemlock boughs out of Skidegate Inlet. Placed in the water in late January and early February just before the fish spawn, the branches become coated with eggs in four to five days—yielding welcome bounty just as winter food supplies are dwindling.

A woman weaves a basket out of strands of cedar root. Haida girls have been taught from an early age to craft all manner of household objects and personal goods, including mats, screens, cloaks, and rain hats, using the roots and inner bark of cedar and spruce trees.

In 1884 an elderly Massett noblewoman warms herself with a
Hudson's Bay blanket while wearing the traditional nose ring and labret, or
lip plug, emblems of her rank. Labrets became increasingly rare in
the 20th century as European disapproval prompted women to forgo them.

The Haida were inspired by missionaries to adopt military-style drill companies and marching bands. The Skidegate Indian Band, shown in a photograph taken about 1913, boasted more than 15 brass instruments and gave regular Saturday-night concerts.

RAISING THE BEAR POLE

On a clear summer day in 1991, the ghostly village of Yan on Massett Inlet, unoccupied since 1890, came gloriously to life. Descendants of the families who once lived there gathered with those from other ancestral Haida communities to celebrate one of their most joyous ceremonies: the raising of a new totem pole.

Not long before, it had seemed there would never be another pole raising in Haida Gwaii (Queen Charlotte Islands). The old poles, precious family crests to the clans who erected them, had been taken by museums and souvenir hunters, cut up for firewood at the instigation of missionaries, or had toppled and decayed. And no carvers remained in the vacant towns—or elsewhere—to replace them. "The art of carving poles," one Canadian anthropologist stated matter-of-factly in 1930, "belongs to the past."

In the 1960s, however, Northwest Coast Indians experienced a renaissance of their own culture, and young Haida artists began relearning the art of pole carving. In 1969 the town of Old Massett—one of the two communities where Haida peoples still resided—celebrated the first pole raising in Haida Gwaii in 90 years.

The opportunity to raise a new pole in Yan came in 1989, when Haida artist Jim Hart was commissioned by the Vancouver Museum to carve a replica of the pole that once stood in the village. Later that year, as Hart was finishing his work—the Bear Pole—Vancouver's sister city of Yokohama, Japan, requested that it go on tour in the Orient. Haida matriarch Dora Brooks, a descendant of Yan's ruling family and, as such, the pole's Clan Mother, was present for the Yokohama opening.

In 1991 Hart brought the pole to Yan. In a daylong ceremony dedicated to the memory of Brooks, who by then had died, the Bear Pole was set in place on the shore at Yan to the accompaniment of the singing, dancing, prayer, and celebration pictured here.

Paddlers hold their oars aloft as canoes bearing the "naang ithga," or respected ones, draw to shore at Yan (left) after the milelong journey across the inlet from Massett. Descendants of Haida noble houses, each of these hereditary leaders represented a separate Haida clan at the raising of the Bear Pole, pictured above, in

Just as their ancestors did at pole-raising ceremonies in past centuries, Grace DeWitt and Bessie Widen (below), descendants of the village of Yan, officially invite the naang ithga of neighboring communities to come ashore. Wearing the helmets and cloaks of the Raven, Eagle, and Wolf clans, the visiting chiefs (right) confer the strength, honor, and prestige of their houses upon the event.

Wrapped in ceremonial wool blankets emblazoned with their clan crests worked in mother-of-pearl and abalone buttons, head pole carver Jim Hart (below, second from right) and his assistants face the shore to sing a song of welcome to the disembarking chiefs. Other than the raven crest, second from left, all of the crests displayed here are those of the Eagle Clan.

A drummer named Guujaaw (above), whose ancestors came from Skedans in southern Haida Gwaii, sings a traditional pole-raising song from the northern part of the islands. At his side is a northern Haida clansman, whose presence at the ceremony allows the use of the song. As Guujaaw sings, the carvers carrying their tools (right) dance around the pole to expunge evil spirits and summon good ones. Led by Jim Hart (wearing a hat and holding a shovel and adz), the dance marks the carvers' final obligation to the pole.

Just before the pole is to be lifted, all able-bodied guests assemble around it and roll it face-down (below, top photograph). Then, pole raiser Ernie Collison (far right, bottom photograph), Haida Nation vice-president and master of ceremonies for the event, supervises the final preparations. Ropes are secured to the pole, a prayer is said, and mementos of Yan matriarch Dora Brooks are placed in the hole.

Having dug a seven-foot-deep pit to hold the Bear Pole, Haida men raise the upper end (inset at left) with tackle that has been anchored 30 feet up in nearby trees. Others steady the shaft with ropes from the sides and a big wooden brace from below (left), until the base slides into the pit and the pole stands erect.

Still secured by ropes, the upright pole soars 36 feet toward the cloud-studded sky (above). The pit at its base is filled in with boulders, rocks, and gravel, which anchor the column and provide drainage to guard against rot. Finally, a young man—one of two assigned the duty—scales the pole to remove the ropes (left). He takes great care, because any mistake will mar the ceremony.

Solemnity gives way to exuberant celebration with a ceremonial song and dance called Marching into the House (near right), part of an old tradition of inviting guests into the pole owner's residence. Carver Jim Hart rejoices with lively dancing, honoring his ancestors with an Eagle Clan dance (lower inset) and leading his fellow carvers in a competition dance (top inset and opposite). The dancing was followed by a feast that evening at Massett featuring gift giving in the potlatch tradition.

3

ENCOUNTERS WITH THE IRON PEOPLE

A wooden mask carved by a Haida craftsman captures the sharp-faced look of the British and American mariners of the fur-trading vessels that plied the Northwest Coast in the 19th century. This sculpture, with its angular nose, trimmed beard, and freckles made of bits of glass, probably portrays a specific captain.

In June of 1876, the Haidas who lived in Massett on the Queen Charlotte Islands were visited by a white man unlike any who had set foot in their village before. In the century since Europeans first appeared in great ships off their shores, the islanders had traded and occasionally clashed with the light-skinned strangers they called Yets-Haida, or Iron People, for the metal the visiting crews offered in barter. But this man carried no trade goods. He came instead promising salvation to the Haida, whose homeland had been shadowed by sickness and confusion in recent years. Not long before, a young Haida named Seegay had crossed by canoe to the British Columbia mainland, where white missionaries were trying to establish Christianity among the Tsimshian. There he had become friends with an Anglican preacher, William H. Collison. Now Seegay lay near death, and Collison had arrived to comfort him—and to prepare the way for the first Christian mission among the Haida.

After visiting with Seegay, Collison went to the lodge of Chief Weah, head of Massett's leading household. Crouching to pass through the oval doorway cut through the base of a totem pole at the front of the lodge, the missionary found himself in the presence of an imposing council, made up of Weah himself, subchiefs and shamans, and assorted commoners. Speaking through a Tsimshian interpreter, Collison addressed them as "chiefs and friends" and said that he brought good words from "the son of the Great Chief of Heaven," not only to hearten the ailing Seegay but also to inspire all those in Massett who were prepared to listen.

Chief Weah deliberated for a while before responding. "Your words are good," he began diplomatically. "We have heard of the white man's wisdom. We have heard that he possesses the secret of life. He has heard the words of the Chief Above. We have seen the change made in the Tsimshian. But why did you not come before? Why did the Iron People not send us the news when it was sent to the Tsimshian?"

Some years earlier, he went on, the Haida had been stricken by smallpox: "Our people are brave in warfare and never turn their backs on their foes, but this foe we could not see and we could not fight. Our medicine men are wise, but they could not drive away the evil spirit, and why? Because it was the sickness of the Iron People. It came from them." Nor was disease the only harmful bequest of the whites, Chief Weah declared. "Now another enemy has arisen. It is the spirit of the firewater. Our people have learned how to make it, and it has turned friends to foes. This also has come from the land where the sun rises. It is the bad medicine of the Yets-Haida." Presumably Collison's gospel was good medicine that would help the Haida overcome such evils. But if whites harbored such "good news," Chief Weah asked pointedly, "why did they not send it to us first and not these evil spirits? You have come too late."

In the end, Chief Weah and his people accepted Collison and his mission at Massett. But as the chief's speech made clear, in doing so they were not forsaking their sense of entitlement. They felt that it was only proper that whites, who had taken so much from them in recent years, should belatedly give something back. Such reciprocity was essential to good relations among native groups, and the Haida still hoped to benefit from trade with whites without surrendering all. When Collison visited Skidegate in 1877, a spokesman there indicated that the villagers were ready to welcome him but would not willingly sacrifice their traditions: "We cannot give up all our customs. We want to give away property as formerly and to make feasts and burn food when our friends die."

In seeking to derive strength and inspiration from foreigners while maintaining their cultural identity, the Haida were responding to outsiders much as their ancestors had. Linked by protected waterways, the peoples of the Northwest Coast had communicated readily with one another for ages. On occasion those contacts had been violent, but at other times they had been friendly and fruitful, allowing tribes to enhance their existing cultures with new techniques and rituals. When Europeans arrived in the late 1700s, the coastal peoples confirmed their talent for adaptation by trading shrewdly with the newcomers and enriching their crafts and ceremonies with goods they obtained. Over the years, however, traffic with whites exacted a steep price—a toll measured in sickness, turmoil, and displacement. In the process, many old ceremonies were abandoned, and the great houses were demolished or left to decay. Yet the spirit nurtured within the noble households lived on. Ultimately, a sense of pride would impel survivors of the great upheaval to draw on their acquired knowledge of white society and its laws and reclaim their native rights.

A Nootka hunter carrying a bow and arrows stalks game in a colored drawing by artist John Webber, who accompanied the navigator James Cook on his pioneering voyage to the Northwest Coast in 1778. The hunter's traditional costume includes a fur cloak, ear pendants, nose ring, bracelets, fur anklets, and a rain hat of woven grass and bark depicting a whaling scene.

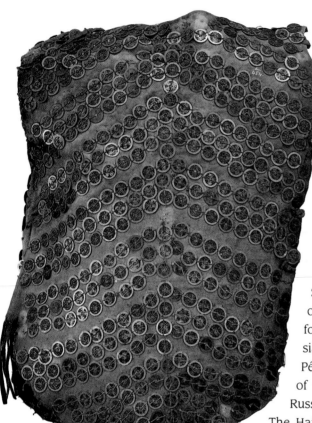

Rows of Chinese coins decorate this Tlingit moose-hide tunic dating from the mid-19th century. Long before then, Russian vessels were trading with the Chinese and returning to Alaska with brass Oriental coins.

For the Haida, the fateful interchange with the Iron People began on a summer's day, July 20, in the year 1774. The Haida inhabiting tiny Langara Island, off the northwest tip of Graham Island, spotted white sails billowing on the horizon. Tall ships were at that time unknown to the islanders, and they had reason to wonder if this were not some fearful apparition from the spirit world. As the mysterious object approached, however, curiosity overcame dread. Indians piled into three of their canoes, carved from single logs of red cedar, and paddled out into the harbor. There they encountered the strangest vessel they had ever seen.

The ship was the *Santiago,* a Spanish frigate under the command of Juan José Pérez. He had sailed up from New Spain—present-day Mexico—to explore the region north of California, where the Spaniards recently had established forts. The expedition had been spurred by reports of Russian vessels plying the Aleutian Islands, far to the north. Pérez had orders to explore the coast and claim possession of potential settlement sites, if necessary, to forestall any Russian thrust toward California.

The Haida declined an initial invitation from the Spaniards to come aboard but made friendly signs. As one of the canoes circled the ship, an elder stood up amid the paddlers and began dancing and singing and casting eagle down on the water—a traditional gesture of conciliation among peoples of the Northwest Coast.

Like other coastal groups, the Haida had a vigorous tradition of trading, and the desire to pursue it soon surmounted their initial caution. The trading began that same day and continued on the next, when a score of canoes carrying as many as 200 men and women surrounded the ship. The Haida bartered sleek sea otter pelts and handmade articles such as blankets, finely woven of mountain goat hair. In return, the Spanish sailors offered clothing, beads, and metal knives. The metal was especially valued by the Haida, who already had a small amount of iron, obtained through intertribal trade from Asia or perhaps from shipwrecks.

While others bargained from their canoes, two of the bolder Haidas went on board the *Santiago.* Garbed in cloaks of animal skins and conical woven hats, the visitors toured the ship and, to the delight of the two friars on board, stopped in astonishment before an image of the Virgin

Mary. They reached out with their hands and touched the painting, Friar Juan Crespi noted, "to learn whether it were alive."

Pérez was not so venturesome. His orders called for him to draw the Indians "into the sweet, soft, desirable vassalage" of the Spanish king, so that they "may be bathed in the light of the Gospel by means of spiritual conquest." But the Spanish captain was inexperienced at exploration and wary of native treachery. He declined Haida entreaties to go ashore and departed after two days without setting foot on land—leaving the Haida on the Queen Charlotte Islands free to live and worship by their own light.

Pérez's brief offshore encounter with the Haida was the first contact between Europeans and Indians of the Northwest Coast to be recorded in writing. Yet various coastal tribes preserved their own tales of early meetings with European sailing ships that may have occurred about the same time or shortly thereafter. The Yakutat Tlingit of the Alaskan coast, for example, told of the first such sighting of tall ships off their shores. When two vessels entered Lituya Bay, the story recounts, the Tlingit thought they were great birds, "perhaps Raven himself." The onlookers fled in fright, but returned to the shore after a while and peered out through rolled-up skunk cabbage leaves, fearing that if they "looked directly at Raven they might turn to stone." A band of Tlingit warriors boldly donned their armor, took up their bows, and paddled out in a canoe to confront the mysterious presences—only to capsize when an awful burst of thunder and smoke from one of the vessels caused them to lose their balance.

Finally, a noble old Tlingit who was nearly blind announced to the others that his life "was behind him, and that he would see if Raven really turned men to stone." He put on a cloak of sea otter fur and had his slaves paddle him out to

A Tlingit frontlet from the early 19th century, decorated with swanskin and abalone, portrays Raven clutching a chest that contains daylight, represented by a mirror. This inlay is thought to be one of the first mirrors ever seen by the Tlingit people.

the ship. "When he got on board," the tale relates, "his eyesight was so poor that he mistook the sailors for crows, and threw away the rice that was offered him, thinking it was worms." But he soon recovered his composure and offered his fur cloak to the visitors, returning to shore a short time later with a tin pan and gifts of food he received in return. Soon other Tlingits were flocking to the ships to barter with the curious interlopers.

Another such legend was preserved by the Kitkatla Tsimshian, who lived across the strait from the Haida. According to the tale, a chief was camped with his people on a beach when a floating island populated by hairy beings hove into sight offshore. A band of these creatures left the island and "came ashore inside a large spider"—a longboat with many oars. These intruders appalled the Tsimshian: The sounds they made were unintelligible, "and most offensive of all, they brought their own food, a shameless arrogance." Unaware of their gaffe, the visitors offered rice, molasses, and biscuits to the Tsimshian, who mistook those items for "maggots, coagulated blood from a corpse, and a lichen called ghost bread." The chief ordered his people to eat the disgusting offerings, "and they complied so as not to give offense to the beings." Reassured, the ship's captain gave the Tsimshian chief some bars of soap, among other gifts, and the two parties were reconciled. In this account, as in the Tlingit legend and the narratives of the Pérez expedition, the diplomatic poise of the coastal peoples in the face of frightful intruders helped foster peaceful exchanges.

Trade between whites and Indians was soon flourishing. It began in earnest in 1778, when the English explorer James Cook, scouting the west coast of the island known today as Vancouver, put in at an inviting bay, where he was greeted warmly by a people he called the Nootka. Unlike Pérez, Cook was bold enough to trust in the welcome he received, and

Crewmen from a Spanish ship gawk at a carved mortuary pole, while Yakutat Tlingits in the background fell huge evergreens to construct more tall tombs, such as those seen at left and right, made to contain the remains of dead members of a chief's family. The drawing was done by Ferdinando Brambilla, ship's artist on a 1791 voyage sent from Mexico by the Spanish Crown to chart the waters off the Northwest Coast and assert claims to the region for Spain.

put ashore. Brisk trading ensued, and Cook carried away many sea otter skins, which he later sold for the equivalent of up to $120 apiece in China. When this coup was publicized, British and American merchant ships began to haunt the Northwest Coast, devoting most of their attention to the southern and central regions, while Russian fur traders continued to dominate Alaska. Between 1785 and 1815, more than 140 British and American ships called on coastal peoples to trade for sea otter skins and a variety of other items. The native zeal to barter manifested itself at every inlet—from the Columbia River, where explorer Meriwether Lewis reported about 1805 that the Chinook would haggle all day over a handful of roots, to Yakutat Bay, where a British ship's officer noted that the Tlingit "stripped themselves almost naked, to spin out their trade."

One effect of burgeoning commerce was to endow white and Indian traders with a common parlance: Chinook Jargon. By the time whites reached the area, the Chinook were master traders of longstanding, who profited by their position athwart the Columbia River to funnel slaves, elk hides, and other commodities from the interior to prosperous coastal tribes. The enterprising Chinook picked up many phrases from the native groups they dealt with, including *potlatch* and *tyee,* or "chief," both of Nootkan derivation. They later bequeathed those terms to whites along with some of their own words, such as *tillikum,* which came to mean "people" or "friend." The lexicon was further enlarged with the white people's words: *Boston* stood for "Anglo-American," because the earliest American trading ships were from that eastern city. Converted Anglicisms, such as *melass* for "molasses," were added, along with phrases that imitated the sounds objects made, like *tum tum* for "heart." Eventually the jargon grew to contain about 1,000 words and outlived the Chinook language proper. A century after white seafarers began visiting the

coast, tens of thousands of Indians and whites spoke the dialect in some phase of their life.

In this as in other aspects of their cultural exchange with whites, the Northwest Indians played an active rather than a passive role. The seagoing fur traders were occasional visitors to the coast, not settlers or colonizers, and as such they did not transform native societies. Instead, they gave Indians the wherewithal to rework their traditions as they saw fit. Spurning the beads that other indigenous peoples often coveted, coastal groups sought useful items from white traders such as iron chisels, from which they made adzes and other woodworking tools to replace their traditional stone implements. By 1800 the Tlingit and the Haida had learned how to forge iron. Improved metal tools enabled native artisans to proclaim the rising fortunes of their households by carving totem poles of unprecedented dimensions and intricacy. Among the Haida and other groups prominent in the maritime trade, the ornate columns rose up to 50 feet, looming over the great houses. Ceremonial life was enriched as well, as European clothing and other trade items became part of the costumes and props used for the dramatic winter dances and other rites.

Far from feeling exploited by whites, many coastal peoples sought ways to prolong their contacts with the traders. When the sea otter population began to decline in the early 1800s from overhunting, the Haida revived their old craft of carving small objects from the local black shale known as argillite. In place of the traditional amulets and labrets, or lip ornaments, Haida artisans carved curios that appealed to the fancies of white seafarers—smoking pipes, platters, flutes, even miniature totem poles, which the visitors carried home as souvenirs.

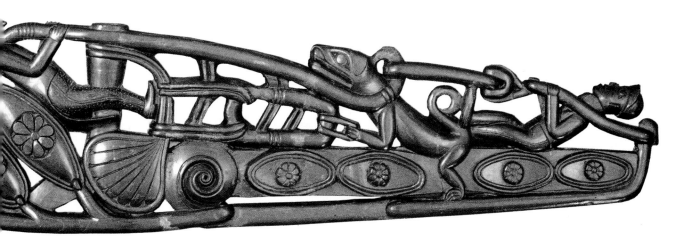

Carved from ivory and the slatelike rock known as argillite, a ship's officer (left) stands with arms akimbo in a delicate Haida statuette made for trade with visiting mariners, probably in the 1840s. Another example of Haida skill is the complex argillite tobacco pipe shown above, which features the figures of two sailors and two dogs connected by an anchor chain. The bowl of the pipe is at center; a wooden mouthpiece would have been inserted at right.

The impact of maritime trade on native cultures was not entirely benign. Keen competition arose among local chiefs for the right to deal exclusively with the visiting merchants, who preferred to reckon with a single figure. Assertive chiefs like Maquinna of the Nootka and Concomly of the Chinook defied the tradition that the village headman was simply first among equals, and eclipsed the leaders of lesser households. Such overlords not only clashed occasionally with whites when they felt slighted by them but also led warriors in raids against nearby villages to claim furs and other booty for trade. The firearms that obliging whites sold to these favored chiefs only increased their advantage over rivals who lacked direct access to the merchant ships.

The toll of such conflict was minor, however, when compared with the impact of the diseases that the visitors spread. The first deadly epidemic of smallpox coincided with the initial contacts between whites and Indians along the coast during the 1770s. The majority of the afflicted tribes were sufficiently populous to endure this initial siege, despite losses of as much as 30 percent in some groups. But smallpox epidemics would recur in the region every 20 to 30 years, as fresh generations came of age with no acquired immunity. To this fearful contagion were added venereal diseases and other communicable ills, whose incidence increased as sporadic dealings between Indians and whites at isolated harbors gave way to prolonged contact at permanent trading posts.

In the early 1800s, land-based fur companies gradually replaced roving merchant ships as the dominant factors in the coastal trade from Alaska to the Oregon Territory. Eager to supplement dwindling sea otter skins with beaver pelts and other furs from the interior, companies established chains of fortified trading posts at coastal inlets. In some places, tribes

HELMETS FOR THE FRAY

The Tlingit of Alaska— unlike most tribal groups to the south—fiercely resisted white encroachment, on several occasions attacking Russian fur-trading settlements. For protection in battle, Tlingit warriors donned helmets carved from solid blocks of wood that represented fierce beasts such as bears and hawks, other animals like seals, and even spirits and ghosts. The helmets were intended to both frighten opponents and endow the wearer with supernatural powers offered by the creatures portrayed.

GRINNING HEAD OF A MALEVOLENT GHOST

HEAD OF A RED-JAWED, SHARP-TOOTHED SEAL

MOUNTAIN GOAT WITH A MANE OF HUMAN HAIR

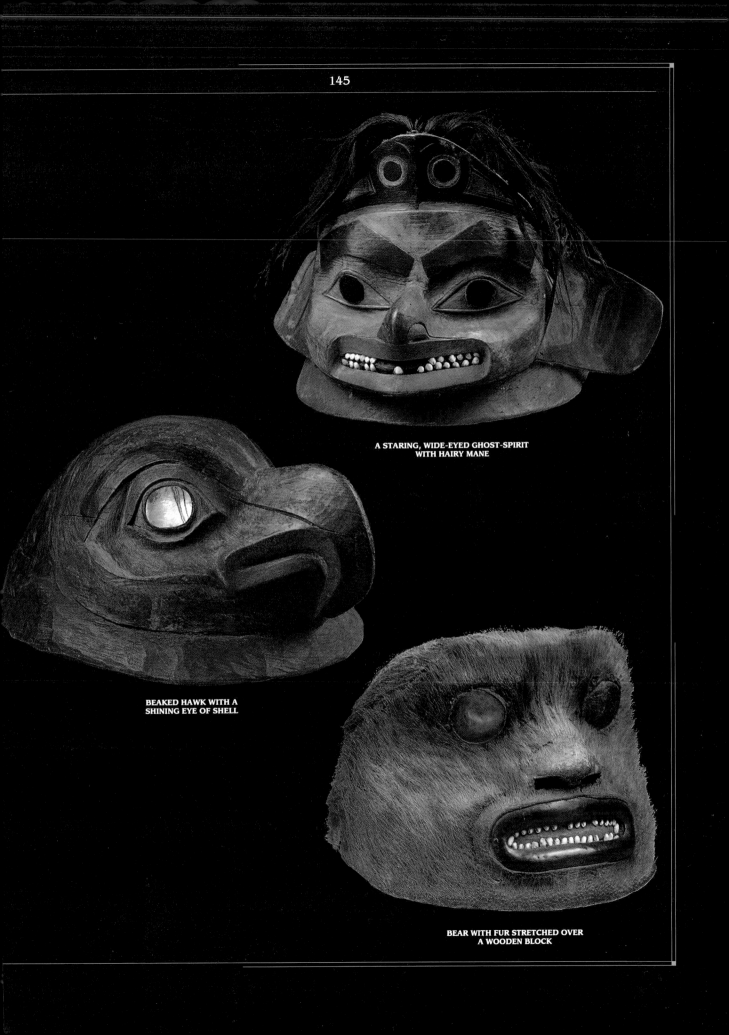

A STARING, WIDE-EYED GHOST-SPIRIT
WITH HAIRY MANE

BEAKED HAWK WITH A
SHINING EYE OF SHELL

BEAR WITH FUR STRETCHED OVER
A WOODEN BLOCK

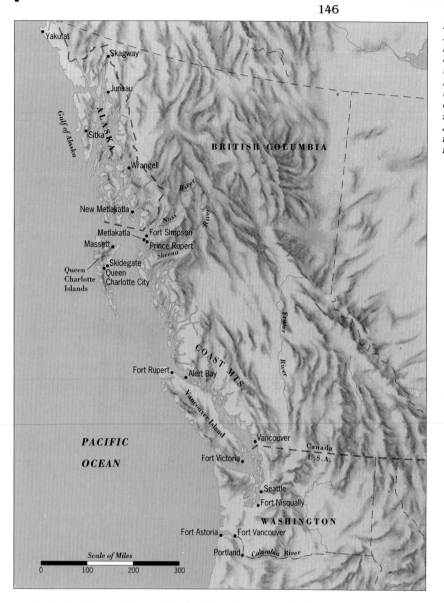

Yakutat
Skagway
Juneau
ALASKA
Gulf of Alaska
Sitka
Wrangell
River
BRITISH COLUMBIA
New Metlakatla
Nass
Metlakatla
Fort Simpson
Massett
Prince Rupert
Skeena
River
Skidegate
Queen
Queen
Charlotte
Charlotte City
Islands
Fraser
River
COAST MTS.
Fort Rupert
Alert Bay
Vancouver Island
PACIFIC
OCEAN
Vancouver
Canada
U.S.A.
Fort Victoria
Seattle
Fort Nisqually
WASHINGTON
Fort Astoria
Fort Vancouver
Scale of Miles
Portland
Columbia River
0   100   200   300

In the early 19th century, Spanish, Russian, British, and American companies established fortified posts along the northern Pacific Coast to compete in the lucrative fur trade. The largest of these concerns, the Hudson's Bay Company, made its headquarters at Fort Vancouver on the Columbia River and expanded north, constructing a string of outposts that stretched into the Alaska Panhandle. In addition to bringing muskets, blankets, and cloth, the traders introduced alcohol, influenza, and smallpox.

resisted their incursions. Tlingits fiercely opposed efforts of the Russian-American Company to build forts at Sitka and other Alaskan harbors. Wearing their traditional wooden helmets and slat armor and wielding muskets purchased from Anglo-American crews who ventured now and then into Alaskan waters, Tlingit warriors attacked and destroyed more than one outpost before yielding to Russian gunboats.

Farther south, by contrast, groups of Kwakiutls, Tsimshians, and Coast Salish welcomed the presence of forts and sought fresh opportunities there. Much of the trade with those peoples was conducted by the Hudson's Bay Company, which outmaneuvered or absorbed rival trading outfits such as the North West Company and eventually established a chain of posts that extended from Taku in Tlingit territory in the north to the Columbia River in the south. Faced with lingering competition from rival trading vessels, the company had to offer high prices for furs, and thus the Indians retained bargaining power. With the sea otter at a premium, coastal peoples obtained river otter pelts from the interior and sometimes tried to pass them off as the maritime variety. George Simpson of the Hudson's Bay Company noted that when his traders rejected a pelt as being too small or dull, it was duly "enlarged, or colored, or pressed to order" and resubmitted by another Indian "as a virgin article."

Indians near the forts preserved their role as middlemen by discouraging distant tribes from approaching the posts and dealing with whites directly. The Chinook warned their native rivals away from Fort George at the mouth of the Columbia River by portraying the whites there "as cannibals and everything that is bad," Simpson wrote. The Tlingit, for their part, prohibited Indians of the northern interior from coming down to the coast except under escort. One inland chief re-

Evidence of the growing sophistication of trade between Indians and whites is the brass token at right, issued by the British North West Company in 1820 as a medium of exchange representing beaver pelts. The North West Company prospered briefly, trading from such small fortified posts as Astoria (Fort George) on the Columbia River, seen below, which was originally built by American fur mogul John Jacob Astor. The concern was soon absorbed, however, by the powerful Hudson's Bay Company.

portedly had to pay a group of Tlingits hundreds of beaver skins for the honor of traveling with them to the trading vessel docked at Wrangell— and for all that, his escorts never let him out of their sight.

Some coastal tribes were forced to appeal to neighbors who had a fort in their vicinity. The island-bound Haida found themselves isolated when the focus of the fur trade shifted from sea to land. Resourceful as ever, they began to cultivate potatoes—probably introduced to the region by the Hudson's Bay Company—and paddled canoe loads of the tubers to Fort Simpson for sale. But they had to deal first with the Tsimshian, who controlled access to the post and expected tribute from all who came to barter there. Rival traders occasionally slipped into the fort undetected, but such forays were risky and sometimes ended in bloodshed.

There was little the fur companies could do to loosen the economic hold of the tribes who surrounded such forts, for the white traders were few and the Indians many. After Fort Simpson was built in 1834, nine tribes of Tsimshians packed up and moved their winter quarters to the vicinity; in time, the native population there numbered more than 2,000. The move enhanced the power of the leader of one noble household whose privileges were already considerable. Known as Chief Legeex, he had inherited the exclusive right to trade with the Gitksan tribe of the upper Skeena River, which gave him control of the richest fur-producing area near Fort Simpson. He soon increased his leverage by marrying his daughter to the fort's doctor. Like other Indian women of high rank allied to company officials, she lived at the fort, attended by one of her slaves. She was later joined there by another chief's daughter, Neshaki, who married the fort's principal official, William McNeill. Neshaki proved to be an avid trader in her own right. Periodically, she would set out in a canoe paddled by her personal crew and barter for furs with Indians upriver.

Such domestic ties with the Tsimshian—reinforced by diplomatic gift giving—helped fort officials retain the goodwill of their Indian neighbors and mediate disputes. In March of 1856, for example, some Haidas managed to gain entry to the fort without being spotted by the Tsimshian, who soon learned of the intrusion and refused to let the Haidas go without paying compensation. Hoping to keep the peace, McNeill invited Chief Legeex and other Tsimshian leaders to parley with the Haidas. "Gave Legeex half a bottle of rum and the others a glass each," McNeill reported, "which had the effect apparently of inducing them to lower their demands." Soon the two sides came to terms, and McNeill soothed the Tsimshian further by offering them some more presents.

Not all controversies involving the proud Chief Legeex were so easily resolved. At many trading posts, Indian warriors made up a home guard that watched over the fort. But Legeex had the power to turn his men against the company, as officials discovered when they tried to break his grip on the fur trade by establishing another post some distance inland. Legeex marshaled his warriors and destroyed the new fort. In the end, the company bowed to the chief's authority and purchased from him the right to deal directly with the Gitksan on the upper Skeena.

Like the Tsimshian at Fort Simpson, the Kwakiutl were quick to capitalize when the Hudson's Bay Company planted an outpost named Fort Rupert in their territory on the northeastern coast of Vancouver Island. Four Kwakiutl tribes converged there when the fort was founded in 1849, creating a native community whose population soon reached 2,000. The Indians around Fort Rupert possessed legendary enterprise. White traders told the story of how, after the fort's big guns were fired to impress the locals, Kwakiutls retrieved the cannonballs and offered to trade them so they could be fired again. The same entrepreneurial spirit drove the Kwakiutl at Fort Rupert to seek furs from mainland tribes and pass them along to the company at a profit.

As the Kwakiutl prospered from the fur trade, they took to potlatching on a scale that was truly remarkable for people who had not been great enthusiasts of that ceremony in the past. Traditionally, only the first- and second-ranking chiefs of Kwakiutl groups had sponsored potlatches, and modest amounts of property such as animal skins, canoes, or an occasional slave had changed hands. But now many Kwakiutls around Fort Rupert were in a position to distribute large quantities of trade goods, in particular Hudson's Bay blankets—woolen items that quickly supplanted the native, handwoven variety. Inexpensive to produce, the Hudson's Bay blanket was readily available in exchange for furs or for labor Indians performed for the company. It soon became a standard for measuring the worth of other goods and gauging the overall value of a potlatch.

The occasions for Kwakiutl potlatches remained much the same as always; when a boy was old enough to take a man's name, for instance, his family had to prove he was worthy of it by distributing gifts. But with the new wealth at Fort Rupert and the intermingling of tribes came added pressure to outdo similar displays by one's rivals. Those expectations were met through generous contributions made by the relatives of the potlatch givers. The proceeds went toward a ceremony so lavish it raised the stakes for all those of similar rank who staged potlatches in the fu-

ture. At some of the get-togethers, thousands of blankets were dispensed.

The blankets themselves were of little significance to the Kwakiutl, but they could be used to purchase objects of great import—in particular, the hammered and engraved coppers that had long been considered among the prized possessions of noble households. Coppers were rich in legend. Some were treasured because they had been claimed from rival groups during the course of daring raids. Among the Nimpkish Kwakiutl who lived at Alert Bay, near Fort Rupert, people told of a copper—aptly named Causing Destitution—that had brought ruin to those who claimed it. The first owner sold it for 10 slaves, 10 canoes, and 10 blankets of lynx fur. The new owner was murdered in a robbery attempt; the next man who possessed the piece met a similar fate. Despite the doom that seemingly awaited all those who handled it, the copper continued to soar in value. "Twenty canoes was its price; and 20 slaves was its price," the legend recounted, "and 100 painted boxes was its price; and dried salm-

Hundreds of Hudson's Bay blankets with their distinctive stripes lie stacked in a house at Fort Rupert on Vancouver Island (above), ready to be dispersed by a Kwakiutl chief during a potlatch. Shown at right is a late-19th-century photograph of Kwakiutls and their village at Fort Rupert, a major trading post and center for potlatch giving.

on not to be counted was its price; and 200 cedar blankets was its price.''

Such storied coppers figured prominently in so-called rivalry potlatches, at which Kwakiutl chiefs competed to see who could give up the most wealth. During these ceremonies, which grew more lavish as campaigns for prestige heated up around Fort Rupert, a chief might display a copper purchased for 10,000 blankets—and worth twice that amount should he choose to sell it—and break off a piece, to be tossed into the sea or given away. His rival was then obliged to do the same to a copper of equivalent value. Few sacrifices were greater for a noble Kwakiutl, but to part with less than one's foe did was to acknowledge inferiority. A man of high rank might also demonstrate his worth by pouring ladle after ladle of precious eulachon oil on the fire. The flames would leap higher and higher, sometimes setting ablaze the roof boards of the house—while the host, near the blaze, looked on with haughty indifference.

Potlatching soon replaced warfare as an outlet for the competitive instincts of the Kwakiutl. Trading company officials discouraged intertribal

fighting, and the Indians themselves recognized that they could gain the distinction they coveted by vying with wealth rather than weapons. Many of the trappings of warfare remained. Kwakiutl tribes planned potlatches as if they were mapping campaigns against an enemy, and their speeches and songs at the ceremonies brimmed with metaphors of conquest. One Kwakiutl term used to refer to a potlatch meant to flatten one's rivals under a mound of blankets. Nobles urged their kin to hoard wealth for distribution as a hedge against similar tactics by their foes: "If we do not defend ourselves," they said, "we shall be buried by their property." The last recorded instance of actual combat occurred in 1865; after that, the Kwakiutl fought with property. Years later,

With his son beside him, a Kwakiutl chief named Tutlthidi prepares to give away a copper in the boy's name. These shieldlike items, crafted from the malleable reddish metal, were symbols of wealth and brought prestige to owners who gave them as gifts.

an elder spoke of the change he had witnessed since his youth, when warriors' blood ran freely: "Since that time the white man came and stopped up that stream of blood with wealth."

If fewer Kwakiutls were dying at the hands of enemies, however, many more were succumbing to disease. Indeed, losses to smallpox and other ills contributed to the potlatching frenzy. As the Kwakiutl population declined from about 9,000 in the 1830s to little more than 2,200 a half-century later, openings were created in the culture's hierarchy. In all, there were more than 500 positions to be filled through potlatching, presenting ample opportunities for the younger sons and daughters of chiefs and for commoners who could make some remote hereditary claim to nobility.

The population decline of the Kwakiutl was mirrored by that of other groups living around trading posts, where smallpox was just the most notorious of the health risks. At many forts, overcrowding and poor sanitation combined with the damp climate to undermine the defenses of whites and Indians alike. Men posted to the forts frequently complained of the long wet spells. "Everyone suffering from dejection and colds," noted William NcNeill at Fort Simpson. "Just the weather to kill anyone who is not made of iron." Around Fort Vancouver, situated near present-day Portland on the Columbia, an epidemic of "fever and ague"—later thought to be malaria—broke out in 1830. The native remedy of steaming in a sweat lodge and jumping into cold water during the alternating spells of chills and fever only increased the mortality rate. In just three years, malaria eradicated an estimated three-fourths of the Indian population in that densely settled area.

Just as insidious as the malaria and dysentery that plagued the outposts were the venereal infections, referred to politely as "ladies' fever" or "large pox." Intimate relations between whites and Indians at the forts ranged from strategic alliances between trading officials and native women of high rank to affairs between the company's laborers and female Indian slaves, whose favors sometimes had to be purchased from their owners. One hired hand at Fort Simpson became involved with a native woman of some distinction and fled the post to live with her. But

After paying some $2,000 for this copper in 1942, a Kwakiutl chief marked his family tragedies and celebrations by giving away pieces of it.

he found to his dismay that her father, like others around the fort, regarded anyone who did menial work there as a slave and treated his son-in-law accordingly, forcing him to cut wood and fetch water. Within a month, he was back at the fort, having learned the hard way that the surrounding Indians were as status-conscious as any white community with an entrenched elite.

Along with the diseases, alcohol did much to disrupt the lives of those who flocked there. Since the early days of the maritime trade, captains had used intoxicating drink to impair the keen trading reflexes of the coastal Indians. In the 1840s and 1850s, the Hudson's Bay Company discouraged the practice in the interest of maintaining peace around the forts. But unscrupulous captains piloting so-called rum ships continued to offer Indians barrels of strong drink in exchange for furs.

Some Indians learned to distill their own rum from molasses. The Tlingit called their product hoochinoo—a loose rendering of the name of the place where they made their first batch of home-brew—and thus gave English speakers yet another term for liquor, hooch. By whatever name, alcohol had an incendiary effect around the forts, where little was needed to ignite violence. In one of many such incidents, two rum ships that ventured up the Nass River near Fort Simpson in March 1862 sparked fighting between rival Indians that left three dead and six wounded.

For all the travails suffered by the coastal tribes that were caught up in the fur business, they remained willing and eager partners in that trade and managed to preserve a great many of their ancestral rights and customs. By the mid-19th century, however, Indians in many parts of the Pacific Northwest faced a fearsome new challenge to their way of life from droves of white settlers and prospectors, who had little interest in accommodating native peoples and regarded the land as theirs for the taking.

The era of white settlement was marked by sweeping territorial decrees whose validity many Indian groups questioned when they realized the consequences. To the south, the lands below the 49th parallel formally became possessions of the United States in 1846 under terms of the Treaty of Washington. The pact arbitrarily divided the Coast Salish in two, with those south of the line falling under American jurisdiction and those to the north coming under control of the British, whose original colony of Vancouver Island would later merge with British Columbia to become a province of Canada in 1871. Farther north, the territory occupied by the Tlingit passed from Russian to American hands with the sale of Alaska in 1867. The defiant Tlingit objected to the deal, insisting that they, rather than the Russians, were the rightful owners of the land and should have been paid the $7.2 million purchase price.

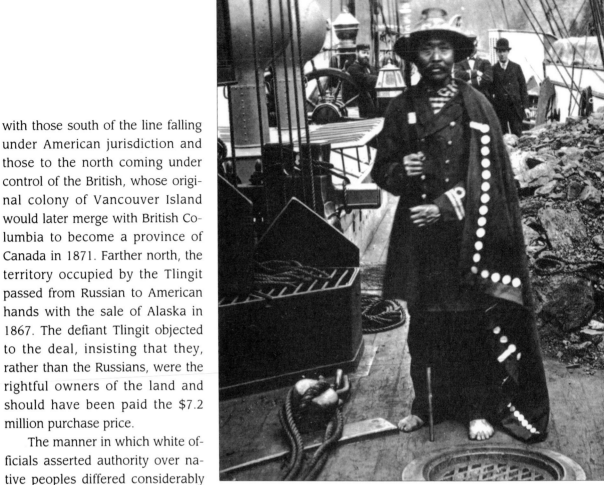

Wearing a mixture of clothing styles—a naval coat along with a button-decorated Indian blanket and a basketwork hat—a Kwakiutl chief stands on the deck of a British steamer during a visit in 1873. The Indians of the Northwest Coast increasingly adopted the laborsaving European dress as it became more easily available in trade.

The manner in which white officials asserted authority over native peoples differed considerably from one territory to another. South of the 49th parallel, more than 3,000 white emigrants had already arrived from the East over the Oregon Trail when the area was claimed by the United States. As always, Indians along the coast did their best to adapt. The Chinook, devastated by epidemics and a decline in the local fur trade, saw the onslaught of newcomers as a chance to recoup their fortunes through trade; some Chinooks even sold slaves to the settlers, who used the Indians they bought to help clear and tend their land. But trade gave way to conflict as the tide of settlers increased in response to the Oregon Land Donation Act of 1850, which granted any adult American citizen a claim to 320 acres, even though that land had yet to be ceded by the Indians.

The task of coercing tribes into abandoning their ancestral lands fell to a militant exponent of westward expansion, Isaac I. Stevens. Appointed governor of the Washington Territory when it was carved out of the Oregon Territory in 1853, Stevens looked on the Indians as barriers to the Manifest Destiny of the white man, and it took him only one year to bully most groups into accepting treaties that left them a bit of land and their ancestral fishing rights. Stevens reportedly told chiefs that if they failed to sign, soldiers would be sent "to wipe them off the earth." He so alienated tribal leaders that many of them later joined in an uprising led by Chief Kamiakin of the Yakima Indians, whose territory lay east of the Cascades in central Washington Territory.

The rebellion soon spread to Puget Sound, where Chief Leschi of the Nisqually, a Coast Salish tribe, made plans in 1856 to attack the burgeoning white settlement of Seattle. Chief Leschi had kinship ties to the Yakima and secured aid from them in the form of a band of some 100 warriors. But Leschi was less successful in overcoming enmities among his fellow Coast Salish, and he could muster only a few hundred warriors of his own. Twice rebuffed by Stevens's volunteers at Seattle, Leschi was later betrayed to authorities and sentenced to death. In time, the Nisqually, like other tribes, had to accept life on a reservation.

To the north, British policy toward native peoples was less provocative, thanks in large part to James Douglas, an early colonial governor who applied lessons in accommodation he had learned as a fur trader. Douglas, whose wife was part Indian, considered Indians "rational beings, capable of acting and thinking for themselves." He opposed removing them to reservations far from their homelands. Instead he negotiated with a number of tribes to buy part of their territories for settlement, paying the equivalent of only a few dollars per family for that land but reserving existing Indian villages and nearby fields for the inhabitants. He soon concluded 14 such treaties on Vancouver Island. When Indians there clashed with surrounding whites, Douglas resisted pressure from settlers for sweeping retaliation. Arguing that it was "inexpedient and unjust to hold tribes responsible for the acts of individuals," he sought out the Indians involved and put them on trial.

Douglas's campaign to reduce tensions between whites and Indians was subverted in the late 1850s by gold strikes in British Columbia. Prospectors flocked to the area by the thousands, many of them from California, where miners had routinely attacked Indians and spoiled their land. The Canadian gold rush transformed the quiet port of Victoria—founded in 1843 as a post for the Hudson's Bay Company—into a raucous boom town, where prospectors haggled for supplies and indulged their appetites before heading for the gold fields. Although the men felt little love for Indians, they were not above doing business with them if the price was right. Large numbers of Haidas, Nootkas, Coast Salish, Kwakiutls, and Tsimshians traveled to the port—the men to trade and many of the women to "earn blankets," as the saying went, through prostitution, a task that fell largely to slaves or commoners. One visitor to Victoria marveled

at seeing Indian women "dressed up as fine as 'White Soiled Doves' do in California." But the lot of the prostitutes was a perilous one, as evidenced by the all-too-common sight of the bodies of Indian women floating in Victoria's inner harbor.

Respectable Victorians tended to blame the Indians rather than their white clients for corrupting the community. By 1859 a campaign was under way to evict the Indians from their camp across the harbor, situated on a reserve set aside for a local Coast Salish tribe called the Songhee but occupied by others as well. In all, there were some 2,000 Indians living in wooden sheds and huts there. Governor Douglas opposed their removal, citing treaty obligations to the Songhee, but events conspired to overrule him. In March of 1862, smallpox reached Victoria, probably by ship from San Francisco. Most of the white population had been vaccinated, but the Indians were defenseless. As the disease scythed through the native

The photograph above shows the port town of Victoria, British Columbia, as it appeared about the year 1870. Across the harbor, in the foreground, is a portion of the Songhee Coast Salish Reservation, which was ravaged by a smallpox epidemic in 1862.

shantytown, local officials panicked, evicting the survivors and burning their huts. The Indians headed home, carrying smallpox with them. Within two years, the epidemic had visited nearly every native village on Vancouver Island and the mainland, killing more than one-third of the indigenous population. The losses left tribes vulnerable to the demands of future governors, who proved far more responsive than Douglas to pressure from whites and who systematically ignored Indian claims until little ancestral territory remained.

By late 1862, the epidemic had swept up the coast to Alaska. Among the Tlingit, only those at Sitka—where the Russians vaccinated whites and Indians alike—emerged unscathed. The dwindling of their ranks did little to mute the opposition of the Tlingit to intruders claiming their land, however. When United States troops arrived in 1867 to take control of Alaska, Tlingit chiefs not only denied their claim to the land but briefly considered declaring war on them. Those plans were abandoned for fear of reprisals, but more than once, American officers aggravated tensions by doing what Douglas had warned against in Canada—punishing entire communities for the presumed offenses of individuals.

One such incident occurred in Wrangell in 1869 after a white trader there was shot to death by a Tlingit seeking revenge for the killing of his drunken cousin by an army lieutenant. The army commander at Wrangell proceeded to back up his demand for the Tlingit's surrender by shelling the native village there. The suspect finally gave himself up and was condemned to death. He told his captors that he bore no grudge against the white tyee, as he called the slain trader. He would speak with his victim in the next world, he promised, and "explain to him how it all happened."

The condemned man's quiet faith that things would be made right after death reflected a new spiritual hope that was burgeoning among the Tlingit and other coastal peoples even as their material plight worsened. Acts of intimidation like that directed against them at Wrangell made it clear to the Tlingit they would never be able to regain power by force of arms. Like their neighbors to the south, however, many were seeking inner strength by embracing new beliefs and reinterpreting old rituals.

Although the Tlingit had good reason to keep foreigners at a distance, they eventually came to accept the Russian Orthodox priests who continued to minister to them long after the Americans claimed Alaska. The holy men had not always been so welcome. When the Russian Orthodox priest Ivan Veniaminov arrived in Sitka in 1834, he found the Tlingit embittered by clashes with Russian traders. After six years of mission work, he could count only 20 converts. But Veniaminov persisted. A tireless cleric who would later be canonized as Saint Innocent, he built the Cathedral of Saint Michael in Sitka, challenged native healers by vaccinating Indians against smallpox, devised a Tlingit alphabet, and preached tolerance. Priests should honor "ancient customs," he said, "so long as they are not contrary to Christianity."

Such policies helped the Russian Orthodox clergy counter the inroads of Protestant missionaries after the sale of Alaska. Orthodox priests encouraged Tlingit clan leaders to assume important lay positions; founded local schools for Indians that provided a popular alternative to Protestant boarding schools; and permitted display of Tlingit ceremonial regalia beside Orthodox sacred objects at funerals and other rites. In time, the round

The Russian priest Ivan Veniaminov established the Cathedral of Saint Michael in Sitka, Alaska (right), during the 1840s and spent four decades ministering to the Tlingits of the region before becoming head of the Russian Orthodox Church in Moscow (below). In common with other Russian missionaries in Alaska, Veniaminov did not attempt to eliminate Indian customs but melded them with Christian observances.

of Orthodox holy days merged with the seasonal cycle of native festivals. By century's end, the memory of Russian traders had faded, yet more Alaskan Indians belonged to the Russian Orthodox Church than to any other denomination.

To the south, Roman Catholicism was promoted through more unusual channels. Although Franciscan friars accompanied Spanish expeditions up the coast, among the most effective early spokesmen for Catholicism were Iroquois Indians from Mohawk villages near Montreal who went to work for the Hudson's Bay Company and other trading firms in the early 1800s. Through Iroquois influence, tribes living in the region of Puget Sound were making the sign of the cross and singing simple hymns well before Catholic priests built their first mission in the area, near Fort Vancouver in 1838. From that base, the clergymen trekked northward into British Columbia, where more than half the native population would eventually accept the faith despite the stringent policies of some later missionaries. Those priests satisfied the Indians' love of ceremony with processions and other pageantry, while discouraging potlatches, shamanism, traditional dances, and other rudiments of native culture.

All such endeavors paled in scope, however, when compared with the model Indian communities organized by an Anglican named William Duncan. A layman rather than an ordained clergyman, Duncan was a former clerk and traveling salesman who trained as a schoolmaster with the Church Missionary Society of London. He combined evangelical fervor with a work ethic so intense that he kept a daily account of how he spent nearly every waking moment so as not to waste any time. When he arrived at Fort Simpson in 1857 to minister to the Tsimshian nearby, he was only 25. But he never doubted for a moment, he commented later, that he would be able "to subvert heathenism, and triumph over ignorance."

Duncan's confidence was quickly tested, however. Approximately 2,300 Tsimshians were living outside the fort in large communal houses whose architecture he admired but whose dinginess appalled him. By dominating trade around the fort, the Tsimshian had amassed wealth, much of which they devoted to a thriving round of potlatches. But diseases were assailing their population, while prostitution and drunkenness were on the increase.

Before trying to reform the Tsimshian, Duncan carefully studied the people and their language. He knew that the Chinook Jargon employed by many traders and missionaries would not suffice for his purposes. So he worked with an Indian interpreter at the fort and became fluent in the Tsimshian tongue. Meanwhile, he visited with the Tsimshian and learned lessons that would make him an effective preacher. He discovered, for example, that the Tsimshian had their own legend of a great flood in ancient times, so he stressed the story of Noah when he later spoke to them of the Scriptures. He was equally astute in exploiting the influence of Chief Legeex and other local leaders. In June of 1858, when he felt ready to preach to the Tsimshian in their own language, he addressed groups of Indians in the houses of the chiefs. A short time later, he taught his first class under Legeex's own roof. By attracting elite students—relatives of Legeex and other chiefs—he made lower-ranking families eager to see their own children attend the schoolhouse he was building.

Despite these initial successes, Duncan soon decided that his twin

This double-eagle crest of czarist Russia, made of copper alloy, was presented to a Tlingit chief during the negotiations that followed the 1804 Battle of Sitka, a conflict between the Russians and the Tlingit.

goals of converting and civilizing the Tsimshian would require a new setting, one that was isolated from both the enticements of trade with whites and the "enthralling influence of heathen customs." In such an environment, he could manage every phase of Indian life and create a utopia. After consulting with Tsimshian chiefs, he chose the site of their former winter village, Metlakatla. Only about 50 converts accompanied him when he headed south to Metlakatla in May 1862. But two days after their departure, the smallpox epidemic sweeping north from Victoria reached Fort Simpson. Hundreds of frightened Tsimshians concluded that

The czarist eagle crest, a symbol that circulated widely in Alaska as Russians established colonial bases along the coast, may have been a model for the image on a Tlingit blanket, elaborately worked with mother-of-pearl buttons and shell plaques.

salvation lay with Duncan and joined his little band.

Metlakatla welcomed all Tsimshians who were willing to abide by Duncan's 15 commandments, some of which required the Indians to abandon age-old customs such as potlatching, shamanism, and ceremonial dancing, along with acquired vices such as drinking. Other rules enjoined the Tsimshians to observe the Sabbath; attend school and religious instruction; and be clean, industrious, and honest. Residents also had to dress like Europeans, forsake clan obligations, and base inheritance on the father's line rather than the mother's. Duncan realized that for most Tsimshians, accepting these edicts was "like cutting off the right hand and plucking out the right eye."

That so many people were willing to comply was attributable not only to Duncan's iron-willed determination but also to traits the Tsimshian had exhibited long before he arrived. As enthusiastic traders, they had been quick to integrate new ideas and techniques into their culture, especially when those innovations brought prosperity—a condition that whites seemed to have special access to. Furthermore, some customs that Duncan denounced as heathen inculcated values that helped Metlakatla thrive. Although he outlawed potlatches, for example, the spirit of cooperation and generosity that these ceremonies had instilled in the Tsimshian lived on—and served Duncan's utopia well.

The influence of native tradition was evident as well in the houses that were constructed at the Metlakatla settlement. Duncan would have preferred to establish single-family units, but he recognized that the extended kinship ties of the Tsimshian people were too strong to be overcome all at once. So he compromised on cottages that resembled those in an English village—complete with shingled roofs and fenced-in gardens—but

William Duncan, British missionary to the Tsimshian, writes in his cluttered study in the settlement of New Metlakatla, the second of two communities he founded for his followers in British Columbia and Alaska. Duncan devoted 60 years of his life to converting the Tsimshian to Christianity.

that were large enough to accommodate a family at either end, with a communal room in between, where, as Duncan put it, the people could indulge their "love of hospitality."

Otherwise, Metlakatla closely resembled a Victorian community. At the center of the village stood the massive cedar church, seating 1,000. To promote industry and self-reliance, Duncan established a trading post and several other enterprises, including a sawmill, a salmon cannery, and a blacksmith's shop. Aside from supporting the community and instilling work values, each of the enterprises paid social dividends for Duncan. The trading post allowed him to control what residents bought, for instance, while the salmon cannery helped keep Tsimshians from being lured away to other such factories starting up in the region. A Canadian official inspecting Metlakatla in 1879 judged it to be "one of the most orderly, respectable, and industrious communities to be found in any Christian country." By then the population had grown substantially, and Duncan had found a way of shielding residents from outside heathen influences. He built a guesthouse to keep visiting Indian traders apart from the locals.

To replace the old tribal hierarchy, Duncan encouraged citizen involvement. Each man was assigned to one of 10 companies that provided volunteer firemen and other services to the community. Each company elected two men to serve on the village council, which also included Duncan and several of the old chiefs. As a nod to their former prestige, those chiefs received half the proceeds from the annual individual tax, which amounted to a week's labor. The rest of the tax went to Duncan to invest in the village, augmenting donations from his English sponsors. Duncan, of course, was the true chief. As justice of the peace, he supervised a corps of up to 40

Its clapboard houses ranged in rigid ranks along the waterfront, the first town that William Duncan established for the Tsimshian, Metlakatla (bottom), faces Prince Rupert Harbor in an 1886 photograph. By then the village, dominated by the wooden church seen below, had a population of some 1,100 and a number of thriving shops.

armed and uniformed Tsimshian constables, who patrolled Metlakatla to make certain everyone attended church, worked hard, and otherwise obeyed the commandments.

Duncan was well aware that the Tsimshian remained devoted to ceremony, and he allowed for various competitions, feasts, and festivals to fill the vacuum created by the loss of the potlatch and winter dances. On New Year's Day, for example, the corps of constables, the fire brigades, and the village brass band paraded in uniform, and leaders gave speeches by order of rank, much as in the old days. After the speeches, cannons boomed, and the villagers sang "God Save the Queen."

For all his authority, Duncan ultimately faced opposition both within the community and without. As a layman, he could not administer Communion, nor did he want to. He feared that the Indians would interpret Communion as a kind of charm and confuse the symbolic feast of the Body and Blood of Christ with their own legends about cannibalism. Duncan's resistance to Communion and his failure to train native pastors fully embroiled him in a dispute with his Anglican superiors, who dispatched a bishop to Metlakatla in 1879. Several Tsimshian chiefs who had long resented Duncan sided with the newcomer, dividing the community. Dismissed from his post in 1887, Duncan obtained a land grant from the United States and moved 70 miles north to Alaska, bringing with him 700 Tsimshians. Settling on Annette Island, they built New Metlakatla, recreating with great fidelity their old utopia. New Metlakatla survived Duncan's death in 1918, enduring as a monument to his leadership and to the powerful communal bonds of the Tsimshian.

Duncan's first model community so impressed other missionaries in the region that some of them tried to emulate it. Methodists made comparable efforts among the Tsimshians who had remained behind at Fort Simpson, while Duncan's Anglican disciple William Collison reorganized Haida villages along similar lines, although he proved somewhat more tolerant of local traditions.

The coastal Indians did not depend solely on outsiders for spiritual renewal. They engendered their own prophets, who revitalized traditional ceremonies. One such movement, the Prophet Dance, began among the Salish of the Canadian interior before the arrival of the white man and later spread to the coast. Its early apostles were shamans inspired by visions. They presided over circle dances dedicated to a culture hero, sometimes called the Transformer, who was destined to renew the world. In time, adherents of the Prophet Dance incorporated elements of Chris-

AN ALASKAN UTOPIA

At noon on August 7, 1887, William Duncan arrived by steamer on the shores of Annette Island, Alaska, to build a new utopia. After years of conflict with Anglican officials, the lay missionary had decided to break away from the church and move his religious colony of some 700 Tsimshians from Metlakatla, British Columbia, to a small Alaskan island that he christened New Metlakatla.

Duncan's freight included a complete steam sawmill outfit, which he had bought in Portland, Oregon, as well as other tools and materials necessary to erect an outpost of Victorian civilization in the wilderness. Residents dressed like British subjects, worshiped in a turreted cathedral, and even performed Handel's *Messiah* in 1907 on the 50th anniversary of Duncan's arrival in the Pacific Northwest.

Despite the missionary's efforts to abolish some native customs, many of the old ways endured, including the Tsimshian language and family structures. Today the town claims some 1,000 Indian residents, who represent the successful blending of Christian and Native American cultures.

Against a backdrop of snowcapped peaks, neat, two-storied square houses line the streets of New Metlakatla on Annette Island. The remote Indian settlement resembled an English village, with its well-kept gardens, city hall, fish cannery, medical clinic, firehouse, and power plant.

Completed on Christmas Day, 1896, the New Metlakatla church had an interior space that measured 43 feet high by 100 feet long. Dual spires reached 80 feet in the air. Visitors referred to the imposing edifice as "Mr. Duncan's Westminster Abbey."

Above: Victorian clapboard houses are clus-
tered around William Duncan's church
(background) in New Metlakatla.

Left: Members of the New Metlakatla brass
band assemble for a concert. In addition to
the brass band, the community had a reed
band, a string band, an all-girl band, an orchestra, and a ladies' orchestra.

Below: Decked out in traditional English
wedding clothes, a Tsimshian couple celebrate their marriage.

Top: The New Metlakatla basketball team of 1922 suits up for a group photograph.

Above: A Tsimshian man attired in European clothing strikes a casual pose in the Haldane Photo Studio.

Left: Six Tsimshian girls model their Victorian smocks and bonnets. One visitor to the community remarked that the "neat maidens in Mr. Duncan's school are as modest and well-dressed as any clergyman's daughter in an English parish."

tianity into their lives, such as making the sign of the cross before meals, observing the Sabbath, and confessing sins.

On the coast, the Prophet Dance gave way in the late 1800s to a new movement that fused Christianity with native customs—the Indian Shaker Church. Its founder was John Slocum, a logger and baptized Catholic from a Coast Salish tribe called the Squaxin that inhabited a region at the lower end of Puget Sound. Born about 1840, Slocum was in his early forties when he fell ill and was given up for dead by his kin, who went off in a canoe to buy a casket. When they returned, they found Slocum alive and well. He said that he had died and gone to the gates of heaven but had been turned away because of his sinful life. God sent him back to earth, he announced, to show Indians the way to salvation by renouncing gambling and drinking, among other vices. He also said he had been promised a medicine more powerful than that of the native shamans. Slocum began to preach to his tribesmen and to neighboring Coast Salish Indians, who were drawn by the reports of his revival from death.

Like the Iroquois prophet Handsome Lake, who had similarly returned from the verge of death to bring hope of salvation to his people, Slocum drew on both Christian moral principles and native spirit power. A year after his recovery, he took ill again, and his relatives called in an old medicine woman. Slocum's wife Mary, who knew that her husband opposed shamanism, left the house in protest and began praying. An uncontrollable trembling seized her, and she returned to the house, still shaking, to pray over her husband. Slocum was cured—because of his wife's shaking, he was convinced—and others

Carved by the Tsimshian artist Freddie Alexei in 1886, a baptismal font, which at one time stood in the Methodist church at Fort Simpson, British Columbia, combines elements of Christianity and native beliefs. The winged male in the blue-gray robe resembles a "naxnox," one of the spirits in the Tsimshian religion that include winged beings.

soon began to experience the same phenomenon that had overcome her.

Here evidently was the new medicine God had promised Slocum to replace the rites of the shamans, and it lent his movement broad appeal. Officials in Washington had outlawed shamanism and other "Indian doctoring," and discouraged spirit dancing. Shakerism provided both—healing and sacred dancing—while incorporating elements of Christianity. From Catholicism came the sign of the cross, repeated three times to open and close every prayer. From Protestantism came simple, rectangular wooden churches, adorned with bell towers and furnished sparely with a prayer table and backless benches.

Shakerism spread swiftly, reaching north to Vancouver Island and south all the way to California. Christian missionaries advocated suppressing the new faith because it was drawing Indians away from their congregations and seemed to mark a return to native roots. The Shakers fought back by using new laws guaranteeing freedom of worship, legally constituting themselves in 1892 as the Indian Shaker Church. It was a wholly native movement, with no ties to the Shaker sect that had spread from England to America in the 18th century. The membership of the Indian Shaker Church would remain small compared with the number of coastal Indians who belonged to the various Christian denominations. But by winning the right to worship as they pleased, the Indian Shakers furthered a resurgence of pride that heartened native peoples of all faiths.

The natural resources of the Pacific Northwest were being systematically exploited by the early 20th century, but few Indians were sharing in the gains. In Alaska, Tlingits were instrumental in the gold rush that began in the late 1800s. They led early prospectors to rich veins of ore and guided the fortune seekers who followed by the thousands over steep mountain passes to new gold sources in the interior. But Tlingits who tried to stake their own claims were denied permission for lack of citizenship. Similarly, many Alaskan Indians were refused employment in the salmon canneries that were starting up—and those who did find work were paid less than whites. Others who tried to subsist by doing their own fishing were hampered by laws that banned their traps and weirs and allowed commercial harvesting at the mouths of salmon streams. Compounding the bias were policies that relegated Indians to separate schools and kept them out of white-owned stores and restaurants, where signs declared: No Dogs or Natives Allowed.

In 1912 Indians intent on fighting discrimination and improving their lot formed the Alaska Native Brotherhood. Reflecting the background of the founding members, who were influenced by Protestant missionaries, the organization sought civil rights that would help Indians assimilate. In 1915 the Alaska territorial legislature offered to enfranchise "civilized" Indians by offering citizenship to those who met strict requirements, such as renouncing tribal ties and securing endorsements from five white residents. Unappeased, Indians argued that they were Alaskans by birthright. In 1922 Chief Shakes—one in a long line of chiefs of that name who headed the leading native household in Wrangell—deliberately committed a felony by voting without having met the citizenship requirements. A kinsman successfully argued his case in court, and the ruling brought Alaskan Indians full voting rights, two years before Congress extended the franchise to Native Americans elsewhere.

In years to come, the Alaska Native Brotherhood led boycotts that forced businesses to stop discriminating against Indians; pressed the federal government to ban commercial traps that were depleting salmon

Carved Kwakiutl masks stare out from a display shelf at a church hall located in the settlement of Alert Bay. After the Canadian government banned potlatches and Kwakiutl winter dances in the late 1800s, some of the Indians were persuaded to turn in objects such as these to local officials.

stocks; and supported tribal land claims in court, culminating in a 1971 settlement that compensated tribes for lost territory by setting up corporations that gave Indians stock in local fishing and timber industries and promoted native culture. In the meantime, Indians who were living in western Washington State had long been waging a campaign of their own against state fishing restrictions. In 1974 a federal judge ordered the state to abide by Isaac Stevens's 19th-century treaties that reserved for Indians the right to fish at all their "usual and accustomed grounds." Within a decade of this landmark decision, the boats from one small tribe, the Lummi, were bringing in more than one-fourth of the fish harvested in all of Washington State.

On Canadian ground, Indians were making similar strides, thanks in part to British Columbia's own Native Brotherhood, which was founded in 1931. One of its leaders in later years was James Sewid, a descendant of Kwakiutl chiefs. Growing up at Alert Bay in the 1920s, Sewid experienced firsthand the galling interference of white authorities in native traditions—in particular the potlatch, which persisted among the Kwakiutl despite a government ban.

In 1921 a Kwakiutl named Dan Cranmer defied the edict by staging one of the largest potlatches ever recorded in the area, featuring such up-to-date gifts as motorboats and sewing machines. Twenty-two of the participants were later convicted by authorities and sentenced to two-month jail terms when they refused to give up potlatch property as ordered. During the crackdown, Sewid's own schoolhouse was turned into a courthouse, and some of his relatives were among those tried there. "The ones who had been sentenced were just kept in the schoolroom and had to sleep on the floor," he recalled. "The mounted police would lock that place up and guard it at night."

Undeterred, the Kwakiutl took their potlatches underground, disguising them as Christmas celebrations or distributing the gifts door-to-door. For young Sewid, the enduring spirit of communal gift giving was a lifelong inspiration. Although drunkenness was not unknown in his community, the potlatch tradition helped to discourage it. "Nobody wanted to have anything to do with a drunk Indian who was just falling and staggering down the road," he noted. Families were disgraced if one of their kin was seen in such a condition, he added, and "they would have to call the people together and give a potlatch to make up for that disgrace." Similarly, the elders at Alert Bay would chide young men for reckless drinking and gambling by announcing publicly that they had squandered

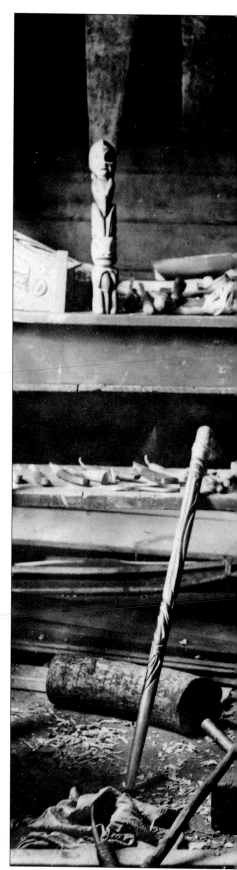

In an 1898 photograph, a Tlingit carver named Yucast holds a speaker's staff he made in his Alaskan workshop. Essentially small totem poles, the staffs were prized as works of art and as badges of honor and authority. In the late 20th century, Northwest Coast Indians were reviving their native crafts and culture after more than a century of dominance by whites and their ways.

their wealth and, as a consequence, had nothing left to give to others.

Lessons such as these encouraged Sewid to live up to the leadership tradition of his ancestors and contribute to his community. As a successful commercial fisherman and a member of the Native Brotherhood, he worked to protect Indian fishing rights and promote legislation that in 1950 finally lifted the ban on potlatching. A decade later, when Sewid was serving as chief councilor at Alert Bay, his uncle honored him at a potlatch. On the last day of the ceremony, Sewid recalled, his uncle called him before the assembled guests and presented him with a "talking stick," or speaker's staff, engraved like a totem pole with family crests, one atop the other. The stick told of spirits who had granted power to his ancestors—among them Dzunakwa, a legendary giantess, who allowed an ancient clansman the privilege of assuming her shape; the double-headed serpent Sisiutl, symbol of Kwakiutl strength; and the resilient Cedar Man, who found shelter inside a hollow log when the great flood struck and survived to perpetuate his race.

Moved by this splendid gift, James Sewid returned to Alert Bay and threw his own potlatch to thank his uncle. "This is not a big do as far as I'm concerned," he told his guests. "It is not like the ones in the past, the real big potlatches." He was proud to say, however, that he had not had to borrow from others to "pay for his name," as some Kwakiutls hungry for high rank had been known to do in the old days. He was pleased to have wealth enough of his own to acknowledge his debt to his friends and to praise the powers carved on the talking stick: "It is the duty of a descendant chief to do these things."

In years to come, Indians all along the coast would find similar satisfaction in reclaiming the potlatch, along with spirit dancing and other customs that white authorities had previously tried to suppress. Pride in the rituals was not limited to those with great ancestors, for distinctions of rank meant less than they did at one time, and villagers had come to regard the noble ceremonies as a communal legacy. Once again, as they had when white traders brought fresh wealth to the coast two centuries earlier, Indian artisans were putting new tools to old uses. In 1969 the first Haida totem pole carved in the 20th century was erected at Massett. Celebrated by villagers who had reconciled Christianity with their traditional faith in ancestral powers, the totem raising evoked words spoken by a chief at Massett to Reverend Collison nearly a century earlier: "Yes, you can lead our children in the new way, but we do not desire to abandon the customs of our forefathers." ❖

Quileute paddlers, some wearing traditional cedar-bark clothing woven by tribal members, power their new canoe along an old 180-mile trade route to Seattle from their reservation on the Pacific Coast.

ODYSSEY BY CANOE

No item of native craftsmanship excited more admiration among early European visitors to the Northwest Coast than the dugout canoe. Hollowed out from cedar trees and painstakingly shaped by hand, the vessels were models of innovative engineering—and indispensable to Indian life. Vital for trading, raiding, hunting, fishing, and just socializing, they also possessed a spiritual dimension. According to legend, the canoe carried the living spirit of the sacred red cedar from which it had been carved.

But canoe building fell into decline about 1900. And by 1985, when the state of Washington started planning its centennial, dugouts were found mostly in museums. One of the planners, a prominent Quinault educator named Emmett Oliver, proposed a remedy. As the Indian contribution to the centennial, tribes would be invited to build canoes the old way and then paddle them to Seattle for a weekend of racing and feasting.

The event, formally known as the Native Canoe Project but inevitably dubbed the "Paddle to Seattle," attracted a score of tribes from as far away as British Columbia. One group, the Tulalip, who live north of Seattle on Puget Sound, sought authenticity by commissioning two tribal members expert in carving and consulting a non-Indian academic authority. By contrast, the Quileute on the Pacific Coast saw rekindling cultural pride as a way to combat drug abuse, and they invited the entire community to participate.

Work began many months ahead. Giant cedars up to 400 years old were felled—after the Indians gained federal permission to cut the protected trees from public lands. Canoe carving had to be researched, crews trained, and tribal members rehearsed for roles in traditional ceremonies. Then the finished canoes departed their home villages and, with ritual and festivity marking the journey, made their way to their destination city.

On July 21, 1989, came the climax of this journey into the past. No fewer than 40 dugouts—from sleek one-seaters to a Quileute whaler with a crew of 18—glided across the blue glaze of Puget Sound to complete the Paddle to Seattle.

On Gold Mountain, a sacred site in Washington State's Mount Baker-Snoqualmie National Forest, professional loggers (left) inspect a 400-year-old cedar tree to be felled for a Tulalip canoe. Above, Tulalips Neil and Danny Moses, flanking Frank Urbanski of the U.S. Forest Service, watch the 200-foot-tall tree come crashing down. The Forest Service allowed each tribe to buy two of the trees which ordinarily sell for $4,200 apiece, for the minimum legal price of $200. A private company volunteered to cut and transport the giant trees at no cost to the tribes.

Tulalip drummers, competing with the whine of the chain saw, pay homage to the living spirit of the cedar tree as part of an ancient ritual. In accordance with tradition, a tribal elder asked the tree's permission before the loggers went to work.

Laying his hand upon the severed trunk (below), Tulalip elder Raymond Moses thanks and blesses the fallen giant. To replace it, members of the tribe scooped out holes in the soft soil and planted cedar seedlings. The log was trimmed to a length of 65 feet for transporting to the Tulalip Reservation.

On the reservation amid a pile of fresh cedar shavings, Tulalip carver Joe Gobin shapes the bow of the canoe with the blade of an old-fashioned handmade adz. The bow was carved separately in the form of an animal head and later attached to the shell, extending the vessel's length to 35.5 feet.

Working to widen the hull, Tulalip chief carver Jerry Jones (red cap), a 25-year veteran of steel boatbuilding, and consultant Bill Holm place a plastic cover over the hollowed-out shell to keep steam in the cavity. During this traditional stretching process designed to increase the craft's capacity and stability, the builders filled the shell with water and dropped in red-hot rocks to create steam and soften the cedar. The gunwales were then spread outward and thwarts were installed to hold the new shape as the cedar cooled.

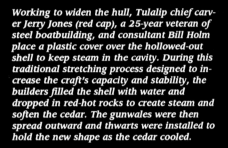

Jerry Jones stirs rocks heating the boiling water inside the shell of the canoe. The rocks were heated the old way—over an open wood fire—but then given bursts of flame from a propane torch to speed up things. During the six-hour process, the canoe's width, or beam, gradually was stretched from 40 to 60 inches, permitting two paddlers to sit side by side.

The Tulalips' adzes and other handmade tools—complete with animal-effigy handles—closely resemble those used by their ancestors.

Resting on logrollers and with paddles ready, the Quileute tribe's newly crafted whaling canoe—a 54-foot-long replica of earlier oceangoing vessels and the largest dugout carved in the United States in a century—awaits its launching. At right, David Forlines, who served as the coordinator of the Quileute project, weaves a traditional cedar-bark vest as part of a cultural-awareness program designed to revive and preserve the old tribal ways.

On the beach of their reservation at La Push, Washington, costumed Quileute dancers rehearse a traditional canoe ceremony, while one of the tribe's new craft makes a trial run offshore. Old-fashioned outfits (below), woven of shredded and oiled cedar bark, afford the Quileute paddlers protection against the rain and cold.

their six-day journey to Seattle, Quileutes at left perform an ancient sacred ceremony, the Snipe Bird Dance, in response to the celebratory welcome from the host tribe, the Klallam.

Elaborate greetings—in the form of ceremonial welcomes from well-wishers ashore and reciprocal rituals from the paddlers—marked the stopovers of various canoes on the journey to Seattle. At left, three of the crews approach shore: the Port Gamble branch of the Klallam (foreground), with Mandi Jones, the chief's 10-year-old granddaughter, in the bow; the Bella Bella Heiltsuks from British Columbia; and the Tulalips. Above, before stepping ashore, Mandi Jones and a costumed crew member perform the dance of greeting while others scatter eagle down, a sacred symbol of peace.

Far from home but with their destination looming within reach, the crews of this little flotilla—craft from (front to back) the Hoh, Quileute, and Lower Elwha Klallam tribes— pull hard to complete their paddle to Seattle.

ACKNOWLEDGMENTS

The editors wish to thank the following individuals and institutions for their valuable assistance:

In Canada:
British Columbia—William T. Cranmer, Alert Bay; Ernie Collison, Council of the Haida Nation; Reggie Davidson, Massett; Guujaaw of Skidegate, Nathalie Macfarlane, Queen Charlotte Islands Museum, Skidegate; Ulli Steltzer, Vancouver; Dan Savard, Royal British Columbia Museum, Victoria.

In Russia:
Saint Petersburg—European House Publishers, Museum of Anthropology and Ethnography, Kuntz-kamera.

In Switzerland:
Yverdon—Maximilien Bruggmann.

In the United States:
New York: New York City—Carmen Collazo, Barbara Mathe, Photographic Collection, American Museum of Natural History.
Pennsylvania: Philadelphia—Dana Flatter, University Museum, University of Pennsylvania.

Washington State: La Push—Frank Hanson, Roger Jackson, Terri Tavenner, Quileute Tribal School; Anne M. Cooper, Tom Jackson, Chris Morgenruth, Quileute Tribe. Lilliwaup—Emmett Oliver. Marysville—Raymond Moses, The Tulalip Tribes. Seattle—Rebecca Andrews, Bill Holm, Robin Wright, The Burke Museum; Mary Ribesky, Seattle Art Museum; Richard H. Engeman, Sandra Kroupa, John Medlin, Gary L. Menges, Carla Rickerson, University of Washington Libraries; Sari Ott, Stan Shockey, University of Washington. Tacoma—Elaine Miller, Joy Wernicke, Washington State Historical Society.

BIBLIOGRAPHY

BOOKS

Amoss, Pamela, *Coast Salish Spirit Dancing: The Survival of an Ancestral Religion.* Seattle: University of Washington Press, 1978.

Bancroft-Hunt, Norman, *People of the Totem: The Indians of the Pacific Northwest.* New York: Peter Bedrick Books, 1989.

Barbeau, Marius, *Art of the Totem: Totem Poles of the Northwest Coastal Indians.* Blaine, Wash.: Hancock House, 1984.

Blackman, Margaret B., *During My Time: Florence Edenshaw Davidson, A Haida Woman.* Seattle: University of Washington Press, 1992.

Boas, Franz:
The Social Organization and the Secret Societies of the Kwakiutl Indians. New York: Johnson Reprint, 1970.
Kwakiutl Ethnography. Ed. by Helen Codere. Chicago: University of Chicago Press, 1966.

Bowman, Phylis, *Metlakahtla—The Holy City!* Prince Rupert, B.C.: P. Bowman, 1983.

Boxberger, Daniel L., *To Fish in Common: The Ethnohistory of Lummi Indian Salmon Fishing.* Lincoln: University of Nebraska Press, 1989.

Bruggmann, Maximilien, and Peter R. Gerber, *Indians of the Northwest Coast.* Transl. by Barbara Fritzemeier. New York: Facts On File Publications, 1989.

Carlson, Roy L., ed., *Indian Art Traditions of the Northwest Coast.* Burnaby, B.C.: Archaeology Press, Simon Fraser University, 1983.

Codere, Helen, *Fighting With Property: A Study of Kwakiutl Potlatching and Warfare, 1792-1930.* New York: J. J. Augustin, 1950.

Collins, June McCormick, *Valley of the Spirits: The Upper Skagit Indians of Western Washington.* Seattle: University of Washington Press, 1974.

Collison, William Henry, *In the Wake of the War Canoe.* Ed. by Charles Lillard. Victoria, B.C.: Sono Nis Press, 1981.

Cook, Warren L., *Flood Tide of Empire: Spain and the Pacific Northwest, 1543-1819.* New Haven, Conn.: Yale University Press, 1973.

Curtis, Edward S., *The North American Indian: Being a Series of Volumes Picturing and Describing the Indians of the United States, the Dominion of Canada, and Alaska.* Vols. 9 and 10. Ed. by Frederick Webb Hodge. New York: Johnson Reprint, 1976 and 1978 (reprints of 1913 and 1915 editions).

Cutter, Donald C., ed. and transl., *The California Coast: A Bilingual Edition of Documents from the Sutro Collection.* Norman: University of Oklahoma Press, 1969.

de Laguna, Frederica, *Under Mount Saint Elias: The History and Culture of the Yakutat Tlingit.* Parts 1 and 2. Washington, D.C.: Smithsonian Institution Press, 1972.

Drucker, Philip:
Cultures of the North Pacific Coast. San Francisco: Chandler Publishing, 1965.
Indians of the Northwest Coast. Garden City, N.Y.: Natural History Press, 1963.
The Northern and Central Nootkan Tribes. Washington, D.C.: United States Government Printing Office, 1951.

Emmons, George T., *The Tlingit Indians.* Ed. by Frederica de Laguna. Seattle: University of Washington Press, 1991.

Fisher, Robin, *Contact and Conflict: Indian-European Relations in British Columbia, 1774-1890.* Vancouver: University of British Columbia Press, 1977.

Fitzhugh, William W., and Aron Crowell, *Crossroads of Continents: Cultures of Siberia and Alaska.* Washington, D.C.: Smithsonian Institution Press, 1988.

Ford, Clellan S., *Smoke from Their Fires: The Life of a Kwakiutl Chief.* New Haven, Conn.: Yale University Press, 1941.

Garfield, Viola E., *The Seattle Totem Pole.* Seattle: University of Washington Press, 1980.

Hawthorn, Audrey, *Kwakiutl Art.* Seattle: University of Washington Press, 1988.

Higueras, María D., *NW Coast of America: Iconographic Album of the Malaspina Expedition.* Barcelona: Museo Naval y Lunwerg Editores, 1991.

Holm, Bill:
The Box of Daylight: Northwest Coast Indian Art. Seattle: Seattle Art Museum and University of Washington Press, 1983.
Northwest Coast Indian Art: An Analysis of Form. Seattle: University of Washington Press, 1965.

Jonaitis, Aldona:
Art of the Northern Tlingit. Seattle: University of Washington Press, 1989.
From the Land of the Totem Poles: The Northwest Coast Indian Art Collection at the American Museum of Natural History. New York: American Museum of Natural History, 1988.

Jonaitis, Aldona, ed., *Chiefly Feasts: The Enduring Kwakiutl Potlatch.* Seattle: University of Washington Press, 1991.

Kan, Sergei, *Symbolic Immortality: The Tlingit Potlatch of the Nineteenth Century.* Washington, D.C.: Smithsonian Institution Press, 1989.

Kaplan, Susan A., and Kristin J. Barsness, *Raven's Journey: The World of Alaska's Native People.* Philadelphia: University Museum, University of Pennsylvania, 1986.

Kirk, Ruth, *Tradition & Change on the Northwest Coast: The Makah, Nuu-chah-nulth, Southern Kwakiutl, and Nuxalk.* Seattle: University of Washington Press, 1986.

Knight, Rolf, *Indians at Work: An Informal History of Native Indian Labour in British Columbia, 1858-1930.* Vancouver, B.C.: New Star Books, 1978.

Lewis, Claudia, *Indian Families of the Northwest Coast: The Impact of Change.* Chicago: University of Chicago Press, 1970.

MacDonald, George F., *Haida Monumental Art: Villages of the Queen Charlotte Islands.* Vancouver: University of British Columbia Press, 1983.

Malin, Edward, *A World of Faces: Masks of the Northwest Coast Indians.* Portland, Oreg.: Timber Press, 1978.

McFeat, Tom, ed., *Indians of the North Pacific Coast.* Seattle: University of Washington Press, 1967.

McIlwraith, T. F., *The Bella Coola Indians.* Vols. 1 and 2. Toronto: University of Toronto Press, 1948.

McMillan, Alan D., *Native Peoples and Cultures of Canada: An Anthropological Overview.* Vancouver, B.C.: Douglas & McIntyre, 1988.

Miller, Jay, *Shamanic Odyssey: The Lushootseed Salish Journey to the Land of the Dead.* Menlo Park, Calif.: Ballena Press, 1988.

Miller, Jay, and Carol M. Eastman, eds., *The Tsimshian and Their Neighbors of the North Pacific Coast.* Seattle: University of Washington Press, 1984.

Nabokov, Peter, and Robert Easton, *Native American Architecture.* New York: Oxford University Press, 1989.

Oberg, Kalervo, *The Social Economy of the Tlingit Indians.* Seattle: University of Washington Press, 1973.

People of 'Ksan, *Gathering What the Great Nature Provided: Food Traditions of the Gitksan.* Vancouver, B.C.: Douglas & McIntyre, 1980.

Poole, Francis, *Queen Charlotte Islands: A Narrative of Discovery and Adventure in the North Pacific.* Ed. by John W. Lyndon. London: Hurst and Blackett Publishers, 1872.

Ronda, James P., *Lewis and Clark among the Indians*. Lincoln: University of Nebraska Press, 1984.

Rosman, Abraham, and Paula G. Rubel, *Feasting with Mine Enemy: Rank and Exchange among Northwest Coast Societies*. New York: Columbia University Press, 1971.

Ruby, Robert H., and John A. Brown, *A Guide to the Indian Tribes of the Pacific Northwest*. Norman: University of Oklahoma Press, 1986.

Samuel, Cheryl, *The Chilkat Dancing Blanket*. Norman: University of Oklahoma Press, 1989.

Smith, Barbara S., and Redmond J. Barnett, eds., *Russian America: The Forgotten Frontier*. Tacoma: Washington State Historical Society, 1990.

Smith, Marian W., *The Puyallup-Nisqually*. New York: Columbia University Press, 1940.

Smith, Marian W., ed., *Indians of the Urban Northwest*. New York: Columbia University Press, 1949.

Soft Gold: The Fur Trade & Cultural Exchange on the Northwest Coast of America. Portland: Oregon Historical Society Press, 1990.

Splawn, A. J., *Ka-Mi-Akin: The Last Hero of the Yakimas*. Portland, Oreg.: Press of Kilham Stationery & Printing, 1917.

Spradley, James P., *Guests Never Leave Hungry: The Autobiography of James Sewid, a Kwakiutl Indian*. New Haven, Conn.: Yale University Press, 1969.

Stewart, Hilary:

The Adventures and Sufferings of John R. Jewitt: Captive of Maquinna. Seattle: University of Washington Press, 1987.

Cedar: Tree of Life to the Northwest Coast Indians. Vancouver, B.C.: Douglas & McIntyre, 1984.

Indian Fishing: Early Methods on the Northwest Coast. Seattle: University of Washington Press, 1977.

Looking at Indian Art of the Northwest Coast. Seattle: University of Washington Press, 1979.

Totem Poles. Vancouver, B.C.: Douglas & McIntyre, 1990.

Suttles, Wayne, *Coast Salish Essays*. Vancouver, B.C.: Talonbooks, 1987.

Suttles, Wayne, ed., *Northwest Coast*. Vol. 7 of *Handbook of North American Indians*. Washington, D.C.: Smithsonian Institution, 1990.

Trafzer, Clifford E., *The Chinook*. New York: Chelsea House Publishers, 1990.

Usher, Jean, *William Duncan of Metlakatla: A Victorian Missionary in British Columbia*. Ottawa, Ont.: National Museums of Canada, 1974.

Walens, Stanley, *The Kwakiutl*. New York: Chelsea House Publishers, 1992.

Wardwell, Allen, *Objects of Bright Pride: Northwest Coast Indian Art from the American Museum of Natural History*. Seattle: University of Washington Press, 1988.

Washburn, Wilcomb E., ed., *History of Indian-White Relations*. Vol. 4 of *Handbook of North American Indians*. Washington, D.C.: Smithsonian Institution, 1988.

Waterman, Thomas Talbot, *Native Houses of Western North America*. New York: Museum of the American Indian, Heye Foundation, 1921.

Wright, Robin K., ed., *A Time of Gathering: Native Heritage in Washington State*. Seattle: Thomas Burke Memorial Washington State Museum and University of Washington Press, 1991.

Wyatt, Victoria, *Images from the Inside Passage: An Alaskan Portrait by Winter & Pond*. Seattle: University of Washington Press, 1989.

PERIODICALS

Blackman, Margaret B.:

"Nei:wons, the 'Monster' House of Chief Wi:ha: An Exercise in Ethnohistorical, Archaeological, and Ethnological Reasoning." *Syesis*, Vol. 5, 1972.

"Totems to Tombstones: Culture Change as Viewed through the Haida Mortuary Complex, 1877-1971." *Ethnology*, Vol. 12, 1973.

Drucker, Philip, "Kwakiutl Dancing Societies." *Anthropological Records*, University of California Press, November 27, 1940.

Emmons, George T., "The Whale House of the Chilkat." *Anthropological Papers of the American Museum of Natural History*, Vol. 19, 1916.

Enge, Marilee, "Treasures of the Tlingit." *Anchorage Daily News*, April 4-8, 1993.

Foster, Mary, and Steve Henrickson, "Symbols of Russian America: Imperial Crests and Possession Plates in North America." *Concepts*, November 1991.

Gunther, Erna, "A Further Analysis of the First Salmon Ceremony." *University of Washington Publications in Anthropology*, June 1928.

Hanson, Charles E., Jr., "The Chinook Jargon—Trade Language." *Museum of the Fur Trade Quarterly*, Spring 1965.

Herem, Barry, "The Curse of the Tlingit Treasures: The Struggle for Possession of the Secret Masterworks of North American Art." *Connoisseur*, March 1991.

Lane, Barbara, "Background of Treaty Making in Western Washington." *American Indian Journal*, April 1977.

Mayhew, Anne, "The Return of the Salmon-eaters." *Beautiful British Columbia*, Vol. 32, No. 3.

Ray, Verne F., "Lower Chinook Ethnographic Notes." *University of Washington Publications in Anthropology*, May 1938.

Smith, Ben, "Return of the Great Canoes." *Native Peoples*, Winter 1993.

Tewkesbury, Don, "A Lesson in Paddling Your Own Canoe." *Seattle Post-Intelligencer*, January 23, 1989.

OTHER PUBLICATIONS

Blackman, Margaret B., "Window on the Past: The Photographic Ethnohistory of the Northern and Kaigani Haida." Canadian Ethnology Service Paper No. 74. Ottawa, Ont.: National Museums of Canada, 1981.

Duff, Wilson, "The Impact of the White Man." Anthropology in British Columbia Memoir No. 5. Victoria: Provincial Museum of Natural History and Anthropology, 1964.

Elmendorf, W. W., and A. L. Kroeber, "The Structure of Twana Culture with Comparative Notes on the Structure of Yurok Culture." Monograph. *Research Studies*, Washington State University, September 1960.

Harner, Michael J., and Albert B. Elsasser, *Art of the Northwest Coast*. Catalog. Berkeley, University of California, 1965.

Jenness, Diamond, "The Faith of a Coast Salish Indian." Anthropology in British Columbia Memoir No. 3. Victoria: British Columbia Provincial Museum, 1955.

Miller, Jay, "Tsimshian Culture: A Light through the Ages." Unpublished ms.

PICTURE CREDITS

The sources for the illustrations that appear in this book are listed below. Credits from left to right are separated by semicolons; from top to bottom they are separated by dashes.

Cover: © Maximilien Bruggmann, Yverdon. **6, 7:** Neg. no. 32950, courtesy Department of Library Services, American Museum of Natural History. **8, 9:** Courtesy The Bancroft Library, University of California, Berkeley. **10, 11:** Vancouver Public Library, photo no. 14059. **12, 13:** Library of Congress, USZ-62-52218. **14, 15:** Notman Photographic Archives, McCord Museum of Canadian History, Montreal. **16, 17:** Neg. no. 42298, photo by Edward Dossetter, courtesy Department of Library Services, American Museum of Natural History. **18:** Fred Hirschmann. **19:** Marilyn Kazmers/SharkSong. **21:** Map by Maryland CartoGraphics, Inc. **22, 23:** © Pat O'Hara. **24, 25:** Library of Congress, USZ-62-52197; Library of Congress; Library of Congress, USZ-62-83577; Library of Congress, USZ-62-101170. **26:** Courtesy Royal British Columbia Museum, Victoria; Winter and Pond, photographers, photo no. PCA-87-248, Alaska State Library. **27:** Library of Congress; National Anthropological Archives, Smithsonian Institution, no. 3091-2. **29:** Missouri Historical Society Archives, neg. no. L/A/0187b—trans. no. 4927(2), photo by Denis Finnin, courtesy Department of Library Services, American Museum of Natural History—British Columbia Archives and Records Service, catalog no. 79170 E-1482. **30:** Courtesy Thomas Burke Memorial Washington State Museum, catalog no. 637. **31:** Washington State Historical Society, Tacoma. **33-37:** Rolf Bettner. **38:** Vancouver Public Library, photo no. 14078. **39:** Courtesy Thomas Burke Memorial Washington State Museum, catalog no. 1-1218, 1-400. **40, 41:** Courtesy University of British Columbia Museum of Anthropology, Vancouver. **42, 43:** Courtesy Royal British Columbia Museum, Victoria. **44:** Courtesy Thomas Burke Memorial Washington State Museum, catalog no. 4562—courtesy Thomas Burke Memorial Washington State Museum, catalog no. 1566. **45:** Courtesy Thomas Burke Memorial Washington State Museum, catalog no. 1-846. **46, 47:** Special Collections Division, University of Washington Libraries, photo by Partridge, neg. no. NA 2554; courtesy Thomas Burke Memorial Washington State Museum, catalog no. 1-1779. **48:** Museo Naval, Madrid. **49:** Trans. no. 4925(2), photo by Denis Finnin, courtesy Department of Library Services, American Museum of Natural History—trans. no. 4926(2), photo by Denis Finnin, courtesy Department of Library Services, American Museum of Natural History. **50, 51:** Denver Art Museum; courtesy Royal British Columbia Museum, Victoria; from the Smithsonian Institution exhibition catalog, *Crossroads of Continents: Cultures of Siberia and Alaska,* courtesy National Museum of Natural History, Arctic Studies Center—photo by David Heald, courtesy National Museum of the American Indian, Smithsonian Institution, no. 14/9081; University Museum Archives, University of Pennsylvania, neg. no. T4-204c2. **52:** Neg. no. 411184, courtesy Department of Library Services, American Museum of Natural History—trans. no. 2390(2), courtesy Department of Library Services, American Museum of Natural History. **53:** Courtesy Royal British Columbia Museum, Victoria. **54:** Winter and Pond, photographers, neg. no. PCA-87-257, Alaska State Library. **55:** Courtesy Thomas Burke Memorial Washington State Museum, photo by Eduardo Calderón, catalog no. 2.5E536. **56, 57:** Courtesy Thomas Burke Memorial Washington State Museum, photo by Edward Curtis. **58, 59:** Adelaide DeMenil—Winter and Pond, photographers, neg. no. PCA 87-009, Alaska State Library—Winter and Pond, photographers, neg. no. PCA 87-296, Alaska State Library; Adelaide DeMenil. **60, 61:** Adelaide DeMenil; art by Wayne Vincent/*Anchorage Daily News;* Adelaide DeMenil. **62, 63:** Adelaide DeMenil (3)—neg. no. 336141, courtesy Department of Library Services, American Museum of Natural History. **64, 65:** Winter and Pond, photographers, neg. no. PCA 87-010, Alaska State Library—courtesy Thomas Burke Memorial Washington State Museum, catalog no. 2291; Adelaide DeMenil (2). **66, 67:** Milwaukee Public Museum; trans. no. 4530(2), photo by Lynton Gardiner, courtesy Department of Library Services, American Museum of Natural History; Vickie Jensen. **68, 69:** Vickie Jensen; neg. no. 329173, courtesy Department of Library Services, American Museum of Natural History—courtesy Royal British Columbia Museum, Victoria. **70, 71:** Vickie Jensen; A7490, Kwakwaka'wakw Button Blanket (Q!GEXTRA) from New Vancouver, Ts!adzis'nukwe' British Columbia, courtesy University of British Columbia Museum of Anthropology, Vancouver, photo by Bill McLennan—Field Museum of Natural History, Chicago, neg. no. 13583. **72, 73:** Courtesy Royal British Columbia Museum, Victoria; A9181, Kwakwaka'wakw Speaker's Staff (YAQ!TPEQ) from Kincome Inlet 'Gwa'yi' British Columbia, courtesy University of British Columbia Museum of Anthropology, Vancouver, photo by Bill McLennan; Vickie Jensen. **74, 75:** A6316, Kwakwaka'wakw Killer Whale Headdress from Sullivan Bay, British Columbia, courtesy University of British Columbia Museum of Anthropology, Vancouver, photo by Bill McLennan; Field Museum of Natural History, Chicago, neg. no. 13597; Vickie Jensen. **76, 77:** Vickie Jensen; A3654, Kwakwaka'wakw Robe in the Chilkat style by Mrs. Mungo Martin, Tsaxxis Fort Rupert, British Columbia, courtesy University of British Columbia Museum of Anthropology, Vancouver, photo by Bill McLennan—courtesy Royal British Columbia Museum, Victoria. **78:** Courtesy University of British Columbia Museum of Anthropology, Vancouver. **81:** Copyright British Museum, London. **82:** Trans. no. 3849(2), photo by Stephen S. Myers, cour-

tesy Department of Library Services, American Museum of Natural History. **83:** Neg. no. 104478, courtesy Department of Library Services, American Museum of Natural History. **84:** Werner Forman Archive, London, Private Collection. **85:** Trans. no. K16495, photo by Stephen S. Myers, courtesy Department of Library Services, American Museum of Natural History—from the Smithsonian Institution exhibition catalog, *Crossroads of Continents: Cultures of Siberia and Alaska,* courtesy University of British Columbia Museum of Anthropology, Vancouver. **86, 87:** Trans. no. 3837(4), photo by Stephen S. Myers, courtesy Department of Library Services, American Museum of Natural History. **88, 89:** Special Collections Division, University of Washington Libraries, photo by E. W. Merrill, neg. no. NA-2616. **90:** Neg. no. 336118, courtesy Department of Library Services, American Museum of Natural History. **93:** Werner Forman Archive, London/Provincial Museum, Victoria, B.C. **94, 95:** Peabody Museum, Harvard University, photo by Hillel Burger, photo no. T723ii; trans. no. 4924(2), photo by Denis Finnin, courtesy Department of Library Services, American Museum of Natural History—trans. no. 3835(2), photo by Stephen S. Myers, courtesy Department of Library Services, American Museum of Natural History. **96:** Trans. no. 3850(2), photo by Stephen S. Myers, courtesy Department of Library Services, American Museum of Natural History. **97:** Trans. no. 3852(2), photo by Stephen S. Myers, courtesy Department of Library Services, American Museum of Natural History. **98:** Peabody Museum, Harvard University, photo by Hillel Burger, photo no. T45ii. **100:** National Museums of Scotland, Edinburgh. **102:** Neg. no. 336801, courtesy Department of Library Services, American Museum of Natural History—courtesy Thomas Burke Memorial Washington State Museum, catalog no. 1-1644. **103:** Trans. no. 3840(3), photo by Stephen S. Myers, courtesy Department of Library Services, American Museum of Natural History. **104, 105:** Neg. no. 336624, courtesy Department of Library Services, American Museum of Natural History; trans. no. 3822(4), courtesy Department of Library Services, American Museum of Natural History. **106, 107:** Trans. no. 4930(2), photo by Craig Chesek, courtesy Department of Library Services, American Museum of Natural History. **109:** Library of Congress. **110:** Neg. nos. 22853; 22891, courtesy Department of Library Services, American Museum of Natural History. **111:** Neg. nos. 22866; 22858, courtesy Department of Library Services, American Museum of Natural History—trans. no. 3833(2), photo by Stephen S. Myers, courtesy Department of Library Services, American Museum of Natural History. **112, 113:** Neg. no. 336121, courtesy Department of Library Services, American Museum of Natural History. **114, 115:** Map by Maryland CartoGraphics, Inc.; John K. B. Ford/Ursus, inset courtesy Royal British Columbia Museum, Victoria. **116, 117:** © Gerry Ellis, inset British Columbia Archives and Records Service, catalog no. 33613 B-3593. **118, 119:** © Maximilien Bruggmann, Yverdon, insets Canadian Museum of Civilization, neg. no. 26665—courtesy Royal British Columbia Museum, Victoria. **120, 121:** © Gerry Ellis, insets Field Museum of Natural History, Chicago, neg. no. A854; courtesy Royal British Columbia Museum, Victoria. **122, 123:** David Hancock, inset British Columbia Archives and Records Service, catalog no. 94055

F-7485. **124, 125:** Ulli Steltzer; James McGuire. **126, 127:** Ulli Steltzer, insets James McGuire. **128, 129:** Ulli Steltzer (2); James McGuire (2). **130:** James McGuire; Ulli Steltzer. **131:** Ulli Steltzer; James McGuire. **132:** James McGuire. **133:** Ulli Steltzer. **134:** Werner Forman Archive, London/Joslyn Art Museum, Omaha, Nebraska. **137:** Peabody Museum, Harvard University, photo by Hillel Burger, photo no. T328a. **138:** Trans. no. 4931(2), photo by Craig Chesek, courtesy Department of Library Services, American Museum of Natural History. **139:** Seattle Art Museum, gift of John H. Hauberg, photo by Paul Macapia. **140, 141:** Museo Naval, Madrid. **142, 143:** Denver Art Museum; A2572, Haida Argillite pipe, courtesy University of British Columbia Museum of Anthropology, Vancouver, photo by Bill McLennan. **144, 145:** Museum of Anthropology and Ethnography, St. Petersburg, Russia. **146:** Map by Maryland CartoGraphics, Inc. **147:** Oregon Historical Society, neg. no. OrHi 53251—Rare Books and Manuscripts Division, The New York Public Library, Astor, Lenox and Tilden Foundations. **150, 151:** Neg. no. 411813, courtesy Department of Library Services, American Museum of Natural History—National Anthropological Archives, Smithsonian Institution, no. 56436. **152:** Neg. no. 336105, courtesy Department of Library Services, American Museum of Natural History. **153, 154:** Courtesy Royal British Columbia Museum, Victoria. **156, 157:** City of Victoria Archives, photo no. 97801-02-791. **159:** Special Collections Division, University of Washington Libraries; Museum of History and Industry, Historical Society of Seattle and King County. **160:** Alaska State Museum. **161:** Peabody Museum, Harvard University, photo by Hillel Burger, photo no. T735. **162, 163:** Special Collections Division, University of Washington Libraries, photo by Hegg, neg. no. NA 2441; neg. no. 42293, photo by Edward Dossetter, courtesy Department of Library Services, American Museum of Natural History—Special Collections Division, University of Washington Libraries, photo by Garfield, neg. no. NA 3538. **165:** Special Collections Division, University of Washington Libraries, photo by Cobb, neg. no. NA 2749—courtesy Tongass Historical Society Collection. **166:** Special Collections Division, University of Washington Libraries, neg. no. NA 2430; courtesy Tongass Historical Society Collection—Special Collections Division, University of Washington Libraries, photo by E. S. Meany, neg. no. NA 4142. **167:** Special Collections Division, University of Washington Libraries, photo by Garfield, neg. no. NA 3542—courtesy Tongass Historical Society Collection—Special Collections Division, University of Washington Libraries, photo by Cobb, neg. no. NA 2753. **168:** A1776, Tsimshian Baptismal Font by Freddie Alexei, 1886 from Port Simpson, British Columbia, courtesy University of British Columbia Museum of Anthropology, Vancouver, photo by Bill McLennan. **170:** Courtesy Royal British Columbia Museum, Victoria. **172, 173:** Courtesy Tongass Historical Society Collection. **174, 175:** © Ron Peltier/Whole Grain Perspective, Winslow, Washington. **176-179:** Dan Bates. **180:** Richard Harvey for Quileute Tribal School—Terri Tavenner for Quileute Tribal School. **181:** Marco Mascarin—Terri Tavenner for Quileute Tribal School. **182, 183:** © Ron Peltier, except top left, Richard Harvey for Quileute Tribal School. **184, 185:** Alan Berner/*Seattle Times.*

INDEX

Numerals in italics indicate an illustration of the subject mentioned.